Mother Teresa:
In the Shadow of Our Lady

Sharing Mother Teresa's
Mystical Relationship with Mary

Joseph Langford, MC

Our Sunday Visitor Publishing Division
Our Sunday Visitor, Inc.
Huntington, Indiana 46750

Nihil Obstat:
Rev. Michael Heintz
Censor Librorum

Imprimatur:
✠ John M. D'Arcy
Bishop of Fort Wayne-South Bend
September 20, 2007

The *Nihil Obstat* and *Imprimatur* are declarations that a work is free
from doctrinal or moral error. It is not implied that those who have
granted the *Nihil Obstat* and *Imprimatur* agree with the contents,
opinions, or statements expressed.

Our Sunday Visitor Publishing Division
Our Sunday Visitor, Inc.
200 Noll Plaza
Huntington, IN 46750

ISBN: 978-1-59276-421-1 (Inventory No. T556)
LCCN: 2007935949

Cover design: Tyler Ottinger. **Cover photos:** W.P. Wittman Limited;
Marie Constantin. **End sheets art:** photograph of the painting of
Mother Teresa's 1947 vision by Cristina Cruz-Parra, reproduced with
permission; photograph of Mother Teresa by John Zierten, copyright ©
by Our Sunday Visitor; photograph of Our Lady of Guadalupe from
Our Sunday Visitor photo file. **Interior design:** Sherri L. Hoffman.

PRINTED IN THE UNITED STATES OF AMERICA

A painting of Mother Teresa's vision of 1947 that hangs in the house of the Missionaries of Charity Fathers in Mexico City

Mother Teresa

Mother Teresa:
In the Shadow of Our Lady

For my Mother —
Whose constant love opened my heart
to these two mothers more:
of Nazareth
and of Calcutta

———◄○►———

Table of Contents

*"Am I not here, I who am your mother?
Are you not in my shadow?"*

OUR LADY TO JUAN DIEGO, 1531

———◅◦▻———

Under Our Lady's Mantle

—◦—

"Stay very close to Our Lady. If you do this, you can do great things for God and the good of people."
— Mother Teresa of Calcutta[1]

You are sitting with Mother Teresa, watching her smile as her loving eyes take in everything about you, feeling the comfort of her strong hand on yours, the aura of holiness around her person, the solace of her gentle words. You watch her tend to the sick and the dying, going out of her way to perform the smallest gestures of care and compassion: the caress on the brow, the squeeze of a hand. You see her in the back of the chapel in Calcutta, immobile and bent in prayer, lost in God. How often I asked myself if I were not seeing in such times something of the Blessed Mother herself, experiencing a glimpse of the Virgin of Nazareth.

When I was with her, I had the sense — one shared by many others, and not only Christians — of being before a living mirror of the one whom Mother Teresa simply called "*Our Lady*"; of encountering a representation in human flesh of her whom painters and poets had sought for centuries to capture by their art. But here was more than a painting or a poem, much more than a figure in oil or in words. Here was a living icon, genuine and deep, who gave freely of God's love no matter how high the cost, who radiated his presence even when she could no longer feel it. Mother Teresa did as Mary had done before her during Jesus' long years away from Nazareth, during his infinitely longer hours in the tomb. Even when the Lord seemed absent to her, she loved.

As those of us who have had the privilege of knowing her can attest, Mother Teresa was someone who loved God and neighbor joyfully through whatever came, who would not have changed her life, as she often avowed, for all the money in the world. Just as we celebrate the joyous fruitfulness of Our Lady's long night of faith that stretched from a crowded Cave to a barren Cross, so too can we celebrate the bright harvest of Mother Teresa's own long "Marian" night, turned endless day. Like the blackbird, she sang her song in the night, that night dwellers might mark the dawn.

She was not born this way; she did not begin by shining in the night, by reflecting the same Light as the "woman clothed with the sun" (Rev 12:1 — RSV). It was over many years, through love and labor, that she was forged by a divine process into an "embodiment of Mary in our midst," as she was described by so many after her death, Hindus included. This process had a simplicity to it, as we shall see. It was this: From dawn to dusk and decade to decade, Mother Teresa's life had been spent, in every sense of the word, in the shadow of Our Lady. Day by day, intimacy became transformation.

During the thirty years that I knew her, Mother Teresa became for me the one book on Our Lady that I could never put down, one that continues to teach me, to fascinate me, to draw me beyond myself into God. You hold here in your hands the fruit of my reading of that book, the lights and lessons I have learned from the pages of her life.

A Light Shining in the Darkness

—◦—

"Mother Teresa? A female Albert Schweitzer with nothing much to say. . . ." That is how the "Saint of Calcutta" has so often been seen, even by those who admire her. Thanks to thirty thousand pages of documents gathered for her canonization, a fuller and more nuanced picture of Mother Teresa's inner world is coming to light. What we find is a grand kaleidoscope of surprising depth and richness, a mix of colors, even of darkness and light, which yield their beauty only by being seen together. To attempt to describe Mother Teresa in a few broad strokes by holding up one or another aspect of her life or work without reference to the whole is to fail to grasp who she was.

Mother Teresa lived with her heart in the heavens and her hands buried in the worst this world could offer. She managed not only to live at both poles of this soul-stretching axis, but to wed them, to make them one in Christ, such that Calcutta became a gateway to Jerusalem. She worked this miracle not only in herself, but in all those she touched — the poor, her own Sisters, and the many volunteers and acquaintances of every faith (and none) who found themselves in her orbit. For all of these, through the challenge of her inward night, she spanned darkness and light, pain and love, riches and poverty, even the trappings of heaven and hell, that we might do the same.

Saint of Darkness or Saint of Light?

Who, in reality, was Mother Teresa, beyond headlines and magazine covers, beyond the easy clichés of those who observed her from the outside? Her admirers saw her as a rare mix of saint and social worker, though perhaps not much more. Her detractors, dissatisfied with her low-tech, nonpolitical efforts at charity, demanded that she provide the poor with the latest in medical science, and that she raise her voice to challenge corrupt structures and social injustices.

Not a few agnostics, along with believers whose faith is not as rooted or resilient as hers, have stumbled over the accounts of Mother Teresa's dark night of faith, seeing it as a spiritual crisis, or even as sign of her hypocrisy. But a careful reading of her personal letters[2] shows that, while her widely publicized but little understood darkness was indeed a challenge, it never placed her in crisis. Just the opposite — it carved out more and deeper space in her soul for the One she loved and served without seeing. Mother Teresa's darkness was not a tomb of spirit but rather a sacred womb from which new life emerged. Her darkness was a crucible of faith, hope, and love in which *Mother* Teresa became *Saint* Teresa. Far from being a stumbling block, darkness became for her a stepping stone. Rather than leaving her bereft and far from God, this night of the soul was her grand stairway to heaven's blessings. "Blessed are those who have not seen and yet believe" (Jn 20:29 — RSV).

Mother Teresa's inner darkness was a hidden laboratory of love. Darkness was the school in which she learned to cling to God even in his felt absence, in which she served the pain of others rather than being lost in her own. As St. John of the Cross, the great Spanish mystic, wrote centuries before her, "*O noche dichosa!*"[3] — "O blessed night" that brings in its silent wake such blessings. Through the rigors of her inner night, a participation in God's own mastery over darkness, grace turned coal into diamond, transforming her fragile human love into something robust and divine, changing the darkness itself to light.

A Beacon in Our Night

"*Come, be my light*," Jesus had asked Mother Teresa at the outset of her mission. From reading Mother Teresa's letters, it is clear that her victory over darkness, as everything else in her life, was not primarily for her sake, but for ours, for all who still dwell in their own "shadow of the valley of death" and for whom she promised to "be light" as Jesus had asked of her.

> *If I ever become a Saint — I will surely be one of "darkness." I will continually be absent from Heaven — to light the light of those in darkness on earth.*[4]

God fashioned Mother Teresa into an instrument that would light up our night at its darkest, by leading her through that darkness before us. He made her a beacon for the rest of us, we compass-less sojourners in a world of shadows. Like the Israelites wandering the desert of Sinai, we need not a direct vision of God but signs of him — signs that lead us on to the next stage in our journey, signs that speak to us in his name, created signs of a still-near but unseen Creator.

Though God has given us many such signs, perhaps few have stood out so clearly on the desert horizon of our day as Mother Teresa. For a modern age hankering for the meat and wild onions of Egypt, with little taste for manna and little patience for the journey, Mother Teresa has succeeded in holding our attention, in marking the path to our promised land. Just like Jesus, who cried out to the Father, "Why have you forsaken me" (Mt 27:46 — RSV), but never took himself down from that dark Cross until he was raised up by the Father he could not feel, Mother Teresa never sought respite or escape, only the means to continue. Her perseverance over fifty long, faithful, and fruitful years shows us that there is a meaning to all that happens, and that there is a God who watches over all even when he is neither seen nor felt.

The richness of Mother Teresa's spiritual world often escapes our first glance, either hidden under the veil of her darkness so that we look no further, or scattered through her talks and letters, like rough diamonds waiting to be mined. What is this light, so important that Jesus asked her to pitch her tent in the blackest places, not that she might build hospitals and high-rises, but so that through her this God-born light might shine? And why send her to "*Be my light*," if his plan was only to plunge her into darkness? Or is there indeed a brilliant, buoyant light about her, a light so bright that it blinds the uninitiated (and blinded her at first), a light that brought her through all, and that God destined for us as well in these dark times? Was her inner darkness a metaphor for, and a map through, our modern-day spiritual darkness? What were the light-laden contours of her spiritual world that she invites us to discover and share, that we might better make our way through our own dark nights?

A key element in Mother Teresa's inner life was the person and presence of Mary, the Mother of Jesus. The remarkable spiritual bond between Mother Teresa and

Our Lady, noted by all who lived with her, was not a side-light, not a peripheral devotion in her inner world, but an integral part of her spirituality and mission. And it was even more: Our Lady became a core element in Mother Teresa's own self-awareness. Our Lady — her mystery, her grace, and her role — came to define Mother Teresa. Our Lady was the unseen foundation for all that Mother Teresa would accomplish in the Church and in the world. And as we shall see, the brilliant light that came to Mother Teresa wrapped in darkness was uncovered for her by Our Lady. It was Our Lady who taught her to see in the darkness, Our Lady who had seen through it first, and at its worst, as her Son struggled for his last breath. It was Our Lady whose faith bolstered and directed Mother Teresa's faith, and brought her to stand and not waver, despite the darkness, at the cross planted in her own soul. And because Mother Teresa's long night made of this cross such familiar ground, she was able to recognize and stand in unfazed service at the crosses of the poor scattered across the globe, on Calvaries that bear no name, but where he who bears "the name which is above every name" (Phil 2:9 — RSV) is ever waiting to embrace and save and raise up.

Was Mother Teresa a saint of darkness or of light? The two are inseparable and inescapable; and strangely, one is at the service of the other. Mother Teresa has shown us that darkness trains and draws our eyes to a higher light, a divine light which in turn illuminates every darkness. The letters recounting Mother Teresa's darkness were not the last word, nor by far her only word. There are volumes of other letters, both personal and general, as well as transcriptions of her teachings and recordings of her public talks, that reflect instead an uncommon light that still shone in her soul despite and throughout her experience of darkness. In the beauty and wisdom of her spiritual vision, so briefly sketched below, we find all the proof we need that this simple nun, who studied no theology, was by no means bereft of light, but was rather a fountain of God's life and light, shining in the darkness.

Chapter One

A Lifetime in the Shadow of Our Lady

—◦—

The Vision of 1947

In September of 1946, on a train ride to her yearly retreat in the hill station of Darjeeling, Mother Teresa experienced a grace that would change her life forever. She encountered the infinite yearning, the "thirst" of God for his children. This was the beginning of her great work. Mother Teresa was shown, and she herself experienced, that the God of heaven and earth thirsts, yearns, and longs for the human race. Not only does he accept us as we are, but he thirsts for us precisely, and especially, in all our weakness, poverty, and sin. Many have understood, in the wake of that vision, that Mother Teresa was serving her crucified Lord in serving the sick, the poor, the dying, and the outcast. But few have known that the idea and initiative of the whole of it belonged to Our Lady.

It was in 1947, at the end of a year and a half of extraordinary and almost daily revelations in which Jesus showed Mother Teresa what he desired from her, that she was shown a vision in three parts, symbolizing and summarizing all that she had been told since boarding the train for Darjeeling. This vision was of great importance for her future mission and that of her Missionaries of Charity, and it deserves our close attention.

In the first scene of the vision, Mother Teresa was shown the painful plight of the poor, and the yet greater inner poverty that was hidden beneath their material poverty. She was shown a large crowd of the poor of every kind, young and old. They were all reaching out to her as she stood in their midst, calling out for her to save them, to bring them to the one Savior — to Jesus.

In the second scene, Mother Teresa saw again the same crowd of the poor. This time she could make out the great sorrow and suffering in their faces. Our Lady was there in the midst of them, and Mother Teresa was kneeling at her side. Mother Teresa was turned toward the suffering children and so could not see Our Lady's face, but she heard her say: "*Take care of them — they are mine. — Bring them to Jesus — carry Jesus to them. — Fear not. Teach them to say the Rosary — the family Rosary and all will be well. — Fear not — Jesus and I will be with you and your children.*"[5]

In the third and final scene, Mother Teresa was shown the same crowd yet again. This time they were covered in darkness. There, in the midst of an anguished crowd that seemed unaware of his presence, was Jesus on the Cross. Our Lady was before him "*at a little distance.*" Mother Teresa saw herself there as well, not as an adult but "*as a little child*" standing directly in front of Our Lady as they both faced the Cross. Our Lady's left hand was on Mother Teresa's left shoulder, supporting her, and her right hand was holding Mother Teresa's right arm, outstretched toward the crucified Jesus. Jesus then said to her: *I have asked you. They have asked you, and she, My Mother, has asked you. Will you refuse to do this for me — to take care of them, to bring them to me?*[6]

These visions encapsulated Mother Teresa's call, in her inner life as well as in her external work, for the rest of her life. Three elements in particular would come to characterize her life's mission: the plight of the poorest of the poor, the ongoing Passion of Jesus crucified in his Mystical Body, and the presence and role of Our Lady at the foot of the Cross. Let's take a moment to look at each of them.

The Plight of the Poorest of the Poor

Each of the scenes began with what Mother Teresa described as a "*great crowd*" of the poor bearing "*great sorrow and suffering in their faces*," and each ended with a vision of the crucified Jesus in their midst. This hidden presence of the Lord in the poor and the suffering, not only of Calcutta, but of the world, in our neighborhoods and under our own roofs, was, in Mother Teresa's estimation, the reason for their singular dignity, their true "*greatness*."[7]

By sharing the image of Christ crucified, the poor had become, even if unknowingly, bearers of his Passion, mirrors of his glorious countenance, a countenance veiled but nonetheless present under the "*distressing disguise*" of human suffering.[8] From the first days of her work, she regarded, and reverenced even, the poor and the suffering as a privileged place of grace, of encountering Christ, of conversion. From that first day forward, as she contemplated and recorded her vision, Mother Teresa would never doubt that in caring for the poor she was serving and satiating her Lord. As she served them, the poor would discover their dignity, perhaps for the first time, reflected in her eyes, and experience the presence and compassion of God in her touch. This was Jesus' own purpose in sending her:

> … *they don't know Me — so they don't want Me. You come — go amongst them, carry Me with you into*

them. — How I long to enter their holes — their dark unhappy homes. Come be their victim. — In your immolation — in your love for Me — they will see Me, know Me, want Me.[9]

Jesus Crucified

Mother Teresa's visions began and ended with the mystery of Jesus' self-gift even unto death, made visible on Calvary and hidden in the poor of Calcutta. Mother Teresa's entire life was directed toward returning the Father's measureless love poured out in Jesus crucified, present in the Eucharist, dwelling in her heart, and hidden in the needy:

The slap on the face; the spitting on His face, the crowning with thorns, the scourging, the removing of his clothes, the crucifixion — putting the Cross in the centre, showing that He was worse than the other two. The burial in somebody's grave, all these and many others, especially the terrible longing to be loved — the terrible loneliness, the terrible feeling of pain for His Mother. All, all these [are] the love with which He loved you and me.[10]

Mother Teresa's answer to the great pain and darkness of the poor, which she would share in body and soul, lay in the mystery of God's thirsting love, first revealed in that abode of darkness and death that was Calvary.

Our Lady at the Foot of the Cross

One sees in these visions the central and defining role Our Lady would play in every aspect of Mother Teresa's life and work. She is presented both as provider and as companion in Mother Teresa's work for the neediest, in "bringing them to Jesus." Our Lady becomes a bridge both between

Mother Teresa and the poor who cried out to her, and between the poor and the crucified Jesus who thirsted for them, who yearned to love and be loved by them.

Our Lady says of the poor, "*They are mine.*" Mother Teresa shared in Our Lady's grace of motherhood toward these neediest of her children. She spent her life enclosed in Our Lady's "*most pure heart,*" even as we see her "*enclosed*" by Our Lady's arms in the third part of her vision[11]:

> *With great love and trust stand with Our Lady near the Cross. What a gift of God. . . .*[12]

It is through Our Lady's presence, as portrayed in this final scene, that Mother Teresa will find the grace and courage to stand at the Calvaries of the world, knowing, with the same faith that sustained Our Lady in that darkest hour, that beneath this mystery was hidden the presence of the Son of God. In carrying out this difficult mission, Our Lady will be Mother Teresa's constant reference, model, and support:

> *As a preparation for a joyful celebration of this Golden Jubilee of "Inspiration Day" . . . I cannot think of a better way than to turn to Our Lady . . . for it was at Her pleading that the Society was born . . . so that with Her and like Her we learn to stand by the distressing disguise of Jesus in the world today, especially in the lives of the poorest of the poor, both materially and spiritually, and thus satiate His thirst to love and to be loved.*[13]

The Secret of the Beloved Disciple

Mother Teresa's vision, as she sees herself at the foot of the Cross with Our Lady, reminds us of the gospel episode from which this scene is obviously drawn, and to which it seems to intentionally refer us back (see Jn 19:25-30). In this passage from his gospel, the Apostle John stands at the foot of the Cross with Our Lady on Calvary. John is the sole witness among the Twelve to Jesus' crucifixion, and the only evangelist to record his cry of thirst (see Jn 19:28). Yet we can presume that he already had a relationship with Mary, who in turn led him to the Cross on Good Friday. We know that John, too, had run away in fear, just like the others, as Jesus had predicted (see Mt 26:31). But John, recognizing his weakness, at some point along the way found Our Lady amid the crowd on the Via Dolorosa. In her he found a love, a strength, and a serenity that surpassed his own, and a heart to open his own to the words he alone among the Twelve would hear. Our Lady brought John to faithfulness, and to witness the thirst of her Son. This is what she did for Mother Teresa. This is what she offers to do for every disciple.

This, then, is a lesson for us. We cannot presume to persevere in bearing our crosses, counting on our own strength and goodwill alone, as St. John had presumed to do. Without an intimate relationship with Our Lady, the command to pick up our cross daily and follow the Lord will prove too difficult and demanding. We may indeed love Jesus deeply, as St. John surely did, or as St. Peter did, warming himself at the fire. But we will fail and fall before the scandal of the Cross when it threatens to touch us, if we face it by ourselves. Without Our Lady, we would be as St. John alone on Good Friday, alone before the crosses of life, oblivious of Jesus in our midst. In times of trial, we are often like the poor in Mother Teresa's vision, covered in darkness, unaware that Jesus is there in the midst of us. Without the fidelity Our Lady gave St. John, the Church would never have heard the words "I thirst"; and without the fidelity she gave to Mother Teresa, the world would not have heard those words, or seen them lived out, today.

So the cycle of grace is completed. Surrounded by the poor, Mother Teresa stands with Our Lady before Jesus crucified. In his thirst for her love and theirs, for her soul and theirs, Christ sends her out to search for those who still wait, "*covered in darkness.*" And the cycle will begin again, going with Our Lady to the poor to find the crucified Lord in their midst and to bring them to him. It is these three — the poor, Jesus crucified, and Our Lady — who rest at the heart of Mother Teresa's remarkable God-given grace and mission.

Chapter Two

Wrapped in Her Powerful Presence

Mother Teresa spent the rest of her life reliving her vision of 1947, consciously present to Jesus crucified under a thousand distressing disguises, and wrapped always in the sustaining presence of Our Lady. She kept herself, in the words of the Church Fathers, "*juxta crucem cum Maria*," mystically next to the Cross with Our Lady. This became for her, as Jesus suggested to Martha and Mary, the one thing necessary (see Lk 10:42).

Mother Teresa and Juan Diego

While little is known of Mother Teresa's relationship with Our Lady prior to her visions or how it developed in the months and years immediately afterward, there are parallels in the lives of the saints. Those saints who lived in a particularly close relationship with Our Lady allow us to see their intimate relationship with her, and more importantly still, how we can enter into such a relationship with Mary ourselves. Among the most important are Juan Diego and Our Lady of Guadalupe.

I had the opportunity to accompany Mother Teresa at various times to the Basilica of Our Lady of Guadalupe in Mexico City, during her visits to our community (the priests' branch of her Missionaries of Charity) at our house across from the basilica. There I witnessed firsthand her devotion to Our Lady, and the reverence in which she held the events surrounding the apparitions made to Juan Diego centuries ago. There I began to see more clearly what Mother Teresa had long since intuited — the deep parallels between Our Lady's role in the mission of Juan Diego and in her own.

In the story of Juan Diego, we catch an intimate glimpse of how the first stirrings of a new and deep relationship with Our Lady can unfold. Juan Diego's touching story, which is part of the spiritual heritage of the Americas, is told in the *Nican Mopohua*, the original Aztec document that relates the events of Guadalupe (paraphrased in English in Appendix Three). As with St. John and Mother Teresa, Juan Diego's deepening relationship with Mary gave birth to a mission of service to the kingdom of God.

In Guadalupe, Our Lady comes to bring the light of God's love into the darkness of a broken people and a conquered culture. Our Lady of Guadalupe, wrapped in the shining rays of the sun, appeared to the poor of Mexico and the New World on the *tilma* of a poor *Indio*. In her own way, Mother Teresa, commissioned to "*bring my light into the dark holes of the poor*," was the same image for the poor of Calcutta and the Third World. Our Lady of Guadalupe appeared carrying the Christ child in her womb; Mother Teresa was told by Jesus to carry him to the poor. Both Our Lady of Guadalupe and Mother Teresa were present not only to aid and instruct, but to live among the poor, the sick, and the needy. Just as in Bethlehem, so in Calcutta and all the world over, Jesus "cannot go alone" without our cooperation.

Our Lady's coming to Guadalupe is the first recognized Marian apparition. Guadalupe opens a new chapter in Church history, in which Mary begins to take a more active, more evident and visible role. As the first in a long history of Our Lady's interventions, we find in the story of Juan Diego a kind of universal pattern of Marian grace, repeated time after time in future apparitions and in the lives of the saints. The almost archetypal nature of Our Lady's interaction with Juan Diego gives us a pattern of our relationship with Mary as her children, and as such it can help us understand how Our Lady was forming Mother Teresa in her early years — and how she still wants to form us.

Formed by Mary's Love

We see exemplified in the lives of both Mother Teresa and Juan Diego four important attitudes of soul necessary for Our Lady to intervene in our lives. Let us look at these in turn.

1. Humility, poverty of spirit, simplicity. This first requirement is characteristic not only of Juan Diego and of Mother Teresa but of all those chosen by Our Lady in her subsequent apparitions. As we approach our own relationship with Our Lady, we must begin here, standing before her in a spirit of simplicity, poverty of spirit, and the kind of childlike littleness without which we shall not enter the kingdom of God (see Lk 18:17).

2. Trust. The second prerequisite is one of simple faith in the presence, power, and role of Our Lady in God's plan, with total trust in her, the trust of a child:

> *"Let each Sister choose the Immaculate Queen of Heaven for her Mother. She must not only love and venerate Her, but fly to Her with childlike confidence in all her joys & sorrows."*[14]

Mother Teresa always held a rosary in her hand, even when doing something else. People would ask her why she held a rosary when she was obviously not praying it. She answered that this was her way of reminding herself that she was holding Our Lady's hand, a hand she had never let go of since her vision of 1947.

3. Humble obedience. The third requirement is an obedient and humble spirit. She who had freely said, "Let it be to me according to your word" (Lk 1:38 — RSV) asks the same of her children. We see this attitude in Juan Diego, who never criticized or complained about the reluctant bishop to whom he was sent. We see it also in Mother Teresa, who, while being called "Mother" by millions and proclaimed "the most powerful woman on earth" by the United Nations' secretary-general, was like a child in the presence of the Holy Father, whom she consulted as often as she could.

4. Contemplation. The fourth prerequisite is the development of a contemplative attitude, in prayer and in life, a sense of childlike wonder at the beauty of God's creation and the majesty of his being, an ability to marvel at his gifts and blessings, and to take nothing for granted.

Entering into Our Mother's Embrace: Three Stages of Grace

The close and intimate relationship with Mary enjoyed by Juan Diego and Mother Teresa is not reserved to saints. We, too, can enter the same pattern of Marian grace. There seem to be three steps in this dynamic of grace, three essential stages in our relationship with Our Lady: encounter, listening, and consecration. While these are more explicit in the story of Juan Diego, they are equally present and important, if more hidden, in the life of Mother Teresa.

Encounter

For both Mother Teresa and Juan Diego, Our Lady was a concrete, daily presence to be met with, welcomed, known, cherished, and learned from. Mother Teresa taught her followers not only to pray to Our Lady, but to live in company with her. Living with Mary implies an ongoing, daily encounter with her unseen but powerful presence. This requires not only faith on our part, but also the willingness to invest the time to draw near to her. Juan Diego did not immediately see Our Lady on the hill of Tepeyac on that December morning. First, he heard an uncommonly beautiful chorus of birds from the hill above him, then he saw an unusual light in the morning sky, and finally he felt a peculiar nudging of grace in his soul. He followed these stirrings of grace rather than going his own way as planned across the footbridge over Lake Texcoco and on to Mexico City. He was willing to seek what was beyond the signs, to accept and to attend to the least indications of Mary's unseen presence before ever meeting her. Such simple signs of Our Lady's presence, scattered and often forgotten on our path, draw us closer, by God's design, to mysteries we cannot see. They are invitations toward a personal encounter with the Mother of God.

One such sign of Our Lady's presence, a unique one, is the image imprinted on the *tilma*, or mantle, of Juan Diego. Our Lady appeared on the hill of Tepeyac in 1531, corresponding exactly to a prophecy that had circulated for centuries among the Aztec people. The Aztecs used a time cycle composed of 412 years. During each cycle, so their belief went, the Sun struggled at night as he confronted mortal enemies among the powers of darkness and the underworld, and rose triumphant each morning, but only achieving a victory that was short-lived and precarious. Any night, according to this cosmology, could be the world's last night. So the Aztecs lived in mortal fear, a fear never quelled but for the few hours of each day's light. To help the Sun in his desperate nightly battle, the Aztecs had introduced the practice of human sacrifice, human blood offered for the survival of the world and the human race. Yet it was believed that the day would come, at the end of one of those 412-year cycles, when the mother of the Sun God, a deity named Tonantzin, would appear to save the Aztec nation and the world. She would give definitive birth to the Sun and restore the fullness of his powers, and so usher in a new era of peace between heaven and earth. Human sacrifice would be no more; the night would no longer rule over the day. The exact date of the end of that particular 412-year cycle occurred on December 12, 1531, the very day the miraculous image of Our Lady was imprinted on Juan Diego's rustic *tilma*.

The *tilma* itself is a continuing sign. This rude and humble cactus fiber, which can last at best for thirty or forty years before disintegrating, has withstood the ravages of time for almost five hundred years, remaining fresh and vibrant in color despite its having been, during decades before the first shrine was built, placed along Lake Texcoco for the veneration of the faithful, uncovered and unprotected. There it was exposed to sun and wind and dust, to the touch of pilgrims by the hundreds of thousands, to the constant smoke of votive candles, and to the damp salt air of the lake.

Those who have visited Guadalupe may have noticed yet another miracle. Enshrined at the back of the new basilica in a glass-covered niche is a thick and heavy iron crucifix, twisted back on itself like a pretzel. Previously, in the old basilica, the *tilma* had been exposed just above the main altar, within reach of the faithful, covered only by a thin layer of crystal. This large crucifix had stood directly in front of the image. One morning in 1921, a Masonic group planted a powerful bomb inside a flower vase and placed it on the altar, inches from the *tilma*. Shortly before the morning Mass, the hidden dynamite exploded, knocking the basilica's huge marble statues from their niches to the ground. The blast shattered the windows of the basilica as well as those of nearby houses. When the dust had settled, this iron crucifix was found to be bent and twisted as if it had been putty in the hands of the heat, yet the paper-thin glass covering the *tilma* and the sacred image itself were intact. Our Lady is indeed still among us, and the power of the Holy Spirit upon her has not diminished.

Pope Benedict XIV, after investigating and approving the apparitions of Guadalupe, marveled at what God and Our Lady had done there. Referring to the sign of her presence left in the miraculous image, he declared, quoting the words of Scripture, that "God has not done anything like this for any other nation" (see Ps 147:20).

If we want to understand Mother Teresa, to imitate her, and to follow in her footsteps on the path to holiness, intimacy with Our Lady is not something peripheral or secondary. As Mother Teresa herself experienced, Our Lady will begin to arrange the events and details of our life as soon as we give her permission. Our life then increasingly becomes an adventure of grace as she takes the reins of our existence and begins to exercise her spiritual maternity. When we live this daily encounter with Our Lady, trusting her in everything, she gradually integrates every aspect of our life, building it around the grace and mystery of her Son.

Listening

Our encounter with Our Lady is only the beginning. If I am her child and she is my mother, she will speak to me. Every time Our Lady appears, from Guadalupe to the present, she speaks. She has something specific to communicate, not only to the world, but to each of us. This will not necessarily take the form of audible words. At times, Mother Teresa heard Our Lady speaking audibly in her soul, but usually it was in the simple receptivity of faith. In this simple prayer she had an acute sense of Our Lady communicating her desires to her. All who lived with her witnessed this. Under the eyes of her Sisters and followers, Mother Teresa modeled the simple ways of living in a state of deep listening to Our Lady.

To attain to this state of listening, we need not only openness of mind, but also docility of will before her. The Old Testament Book of Wisdom calls for this kind of docility in passages in which Wisdom is personified, playing a role that the Church has always recognized as that of Our Lady:

> I pleaded and the spirit of Wisdom came to me.
> I preferred her to scepter and throne,
> And deemed riches nothing in comparison with
>   her. . . .
> Yet all good things together came to me in her
>   company,
> and countless riches at her hands;
> And I rejoiced in them all, because Wisdom is their
>   leader,

though I had not known that she is the mother of
   these.
Simply I learned about her, and ungrudgingly do I
   share —
her riches I do not hide away;
For to men she is an unfailing treasure;
those who gain this treasure win the friendship of
   God. . . .
For she is fairer than the sun
and surpasses every constellation of the stars.
Compared to light, she takes precedence.

(Wis 7:7-8, 11-14, 29 — NAB)

Listening to Our Lady requires deep faith in her involvement in my life, in her concrete plan for me. Just as she had for Mother Teresa and Juan Diego, Our Lady has a plan for my life as well. She is not present simply to give a little boost to my spiritual life. She is the one given responsibility by the Father for my growth in the knowledge and grace of Jesus.

I must listen to her voice, the voice of Wisdom, daily, not just once a year on a retreat, or in those occasional moments when I am so moved. If I accept her love for me, if I accept the fact that she has chosen me, then she and the grace of God will do "great things for me" (Lk 1:49 — RSV). Though both Juan Diego and Mother Teresa first said "No, not me," to Our Lady, insisting that they were not good enough or strong enough, in the end they chose to trust in her intercession and in God's power, and miracles of grace began to take place in their lives. We, too, need an awareness, both of our nothingness and also of the fact that she loves us and chooses us in God's name. Instead of looking at ourselves, we can gaze upon her at our side and can say: "Here I am . . . send me!" (Is 6:8 — NAB). Nothing in us surprises or repels her. Instead, she wraps us in her love and sends us out to build our corner of the kingdom.

Consecration

This final step of consecration, or entrustment, involves the gift of self to Our Lady, entrusting all that one has and is into her hands. Entrustment to Our Lady has often been called the "secret of the saints," who recommended handing over to her in a solemn and formal way our gifts and talents, our tasks and responsibilities, and all the details of our daily life.

The story of Guadalupe offers a simple and symbolic representation of the dynamics of Marian consecration. After Juan Diego is told to ask the heavenly apparition for a miraculous sign, Our Lady sends him to the top of Tepeyac hill. She instructs him to collect the Castilian roses that he will find miraculously growing there despite the winter season. Interestingly, Our Lady tells Juan Diego to bring them to her, so that she may carefully arrange the roses in his mantle before he presents them to the bishop in Mexico City.

These roses, given by God and arranged by Our Lady, represent the gifts God has entrusted to each of us, beginning with the gift of life. Our Lady takes these gifts along with the details of our lives and arranges them, directing and caring for them in a way that we would be unable to do on our own. She invites us to allow her to dispose of our talents and the circumstances of every day. As with the roses of Juan Diego, she will prune them, remove their thorns, and arrange them as only she can. This is what allowed Mother Teresa to put herself entirely at Our Lady's disposal, every day.

Mother Teresa allowed Our Lady to prepare and arrange all within and around her, and she entrusted her entire future to her care. This is why, though she faced trials and problems of every kind, Mother Teresa never worried. All was left to Our Lady, the one who had said so tenderly to Juan Diego:

> "Listen and keep in your heart, my littlest son: There is nothing for you to fear, let nothing afflict you. Let not your face or your heart be worried. Do not fear this sickness or any other illness. Let nothing worry or afflict you. Am I not here, I who am your mother? Are you not in my shadow, under my protection? Am I not the fountain of your joy? Are you not in the fold of my mantle, in my crossed arms? Is there anything else you need? Don't let anything afflict you or perturb you."

There is need for an interior discipline here. We need to give to Our Lady, repeatedly through the day and over the course of the years, our worries, doubts, pains, problems, and all self-reference. This is the key, the last step that will bring full relationship with her and allow her fully to intervene in our lives, to act on our behalf as she did for Mother Teresa, for Juan Diego, and for many other hidden ones whom history will never know. Without this commitment, without the gift of our willing permission, Mary is not free to act. But once we take even the first halting steps of consecration, Our Lady begins to enter our lives in a perceptible way. Her goal is to fashion our soul after the pattern God first established in her own, to see us transformed into a living temple of the

Lord, an Ark of the Covenant, that we might carry Christ to the world. This is who Our Lady was. This is who Mother Teresa was. This is who we can be, with her help.

Chapter Three

The Gift of Our Lady's Heart

"Beg Our Lady to keep us in her Most Pure Heart so that we may love Jesus with an undivided love, an immaculate love like hers."

— Mother Teresa of Calcutta[15]

From the Beginning, Our Lady

Mother Teresa's convictions on Our Lady's role in her life and mission can be seen already at work in the opening paragraphs of her Original Rule Explanation. These provide us with a view of Mother Teresa's relationship to Our Lady at the very outset of her work, a relationship that would grow in understanding and depth as the years progressed, but one already built on solid and clear foundations from the beginning:

> *"That the Society may more easily attain its end, let each Sister choose the Immaculate Queen of Heaven for her Mother. She must not only love and venerate Her, but fly to Her with child like Confidence in all her joys & sorrows.*
>
> *"We must imitate her virtues and abandon ourselves completely into her hands.*
>
> *"With Mary, we make more progress in the love of Jesus in one month than we make in years while living less united to this good Mother (de Montfort).*[16]

Toward the end of Mother Teresa's life, I had the chance to witness just how much the presence of Our Lady had meant to her, and how decisive it had been for her understanding of her call. It was early 1996, and her Sisters were preparing to celebrate the fiftieth anniversary of Mother Teresa's Inspiration Day vision in Washington, D.C. After the festivities and a quick breakfast, we went to the airport and caught a plane for Tijuana, Mexico, where the priests' branch of the Missionaries of Charity is based. Shortly after takeoff, Mother Teresa began gazing out the window, lost in thought. She turned to me occasionally with comments that told me that she was recalling that distant September 10 when she had experienced her vision on the train to Darjeeling. At a certain point, while still looking out the window, she said quietly, *"If Our Lady had not been there with me that day, I never would have known what Jesus meant when he said, 'I thirst'. . . ."*

> *Just think God is thirsting — and you and I come forward to satiate His Thirst. Just think of that! So the better we understand, the better we will satiate His Thirst for love of souls. Pray in a special way to Our Lady to explain this to us.*[17]

Our Lady's inner world, and her intimate experience of her Son, lived on Calvary and continued from heaven, became ever more the sacred space in which Mother Teresa lived. She referred to this mystery simply as Our Lady's heart. It was the spiritual atmosphere in which she would live and pray and serve. It was there that she would find her place at the foot of the Cross, and her place in the Church. Mother Teresa understood from experience that Our Lady's presence at her side in the slums of Calcutta somehow purified things no matter how sullied, and beautified things no matter how unlovely. Mary transformed the seemingly unreachable, opening the blackest and bleakest of horizons to the dawning of God's grace.

Mother Teresa taught her Sisters and co-workers that Our Lady's was a presence that helps us to see through the darkness, a presence that consoles and sustains us when we are weak, a presence that reminds us of the cry of her Son when we are forgetting him or following the voice of ego. Reflecting on the strength she found in this Marian milieu, Mother Teresa coined a short prayer that she taught her Sisters: "*Keep us in your most pure heart.*" She was convinced that in this sacred place, all God wanted for her and from her would be realized.

The Immaculate Heart of Mary

When Mother Teresa speaks of Our Lady's Immaculate Heart, she is pointing to the perfection of Mary's love. How often she would speak of the desire to give "*undivided love*" to God and neighbor. The only one who had done this fully was Our Lady; she is the model, the goal, and the grace-filled means to achieve this ideal. Mother Teresa saw the heart of Our Lady as a model of all the virtues she held dear: poverty of spirit, humility, silence, thoughtfulness, haste in service.

Understandably then, Mother Teresa chose Our Lady's Immaculate Heart as her patroness, and established its feast day as the titular feast of her religious order. While other Marian feasts celebrate some single event in the unfolding of Our Lady's life, the feast of her Immaculate Heart points precisely to her inner life; not to something she did, but to the love with which she did everything. In the heart of Our Lady, Mother Teresa found a path and portal into the mystery of Jesus' love for us. The heart of Our Lady represented for her mankind's maximum response to God, our highest and fullest response to his thirst to love and be loved.

The Immaculate Heart of Mary refers not only to Our Lady's love and virtues, but also to her interior emptiness of self in imitation of Christ who "emptied himself" to save the human race. Our Lady's heart is the most empty of all human hearts, the most empty of self and empty of pride, and therefore the most ready to give a heart's welcome and shelter to those who are shelterless. Mother Teresa saw this as the condition both for receiving and giving God to the full.

The Home for the Dying

The mystery of Our Lady's Immaculate Heart is everywhere in Mother Teresa's world, in her writings, her prayers, her instructions to her Sisters, depicted on the back wall of all of her chapels. But perhaps nowhere is that title and mystery more prominent than on the grounds of Kali Temple, dedicated to Hinduism's goddess of death and destruction.

Mother Teresa named this first and most personally beloved of her works, her Home for the Dying in Calcutta, "Nirmal Hriday," "Place of the Pure Heart." This pilgrim rest-home, built in the shadow of Kali Temple, was transformed by Mother Teresa and her Sisters into a refuge for the thousands who had lived their entire lives on Calcutta's streets and sidewalks, and who now faced the lonely prospect of dying in those same streets, accompanied only by a dusty procession of pedestrians' feet. Here, those who had lived like animals on the street, alone and unloved, could "*die like angels, loved and cared for.*" This special Home bore not only the title but also the mystery of Our Lady's heart. For Mary is God's own Nirmal Hridoy, his own Place of the Pure Heart.

Our Lady is that pilgrim rest-house of God's compassion. It is she who offers shelter to succor our poverty, our despair, our dying. She opens her heart to us, as Nirmal Hridoy opened its doors to the destitute of Calcutta. As with Nirmal Hridoy, the heart of Mary is peace in turmoil, consolation in suffering, the promise of new life in our poverty, the presence of God. Her heart is hope for us, hope that we can not only die but also live like angels, spreading the love we have received.

Mother Teresa and her followers (ourselves included) are called to continue that image, to continue the mystery of Our Lady, staying close to her that we might ourselves become a Place of the Pure Heart for God and for others. Mother Teresa saw the humble works of love for the poor performed by her Sisters as a reflection of Our Lady's heart in the world today.

Chapter Four

All Her Confidence

To understand how complete was Mother Teresa's confidence in Mary's intercession and aid, we need to return to the months immediately following her first vision. After Mother Teresa told her provincial superior of her extraordinary experience on the train to Darjeeling, and of her desire to go into the slums to serve the poor, the mother provincial thought she might dissuade Sister Teresa from pursuing her idea by sending her away from Calcutta, far from the slums where she dreamt of serving.

Sister Teresa was sent to Asansol, in another part of West Bengal, where, unknown to her superiors, her extraordinary graces continued. It was during this period that Jesus instructed her, usually in intimate dialogues that took place after Communion, concerning his desires for her and for the work she was to undertake, including such details as the name of her new community, the soon-to-be-founded Missionaries of Charity. After a year and a half, presuming that time and distance would have freed Sister Teresa of her strange ideas, she was brought back to Calcutta, where she returned to her former job as headmistress of the Bengali-speaking girls' school run by the Sisters of Loreto.

Through a series of providential interventions on the part of ecclesiastical authorities in India and in Rome, Sister Teresa unexpectedly received permission to leave her community, to live outside the convent on her own and without her habit while still keeping her religious vows, and to begin her mission work in the slums. To prepare herself for her new work, Mother Teresa left Calcutta once again to spend time with the Medical Missionary Sisters in Patna, where she learned the rudiments of caring for the sick and dying. It was upon her return to Calcutta from her brief course in medicine that she began wearing the white and blue-bordered sari that would become her trademark.

One of her first acts in her new habit was a visit to her former spiritual director, Father Julien Henry, S.J., in whom she had confided her dreams of working with the poor. Father Henry had known of her love for the poor, but he knew nothing of her special inspirations. When Mother Teresa appeared in his office dressed in her sari, Father Henry did not at first recognize her. They spoke together of events that had transpired since he had seen her last, especially what had taken place in the secrecy of her soul. Mother Teresa had little more than forty-five minutes to explain all that had happened, all her plans and her hopes, and how she would go about her bold new project at the behest of Jesus.

Father Henry quizzed her about the future. How would she overcome the enormous challenges that awaited her, a European woman alone in the bowels of Calcutta, with no money and no plan? She answered his questions as best she could, and they parted. Father Henry had been struck not so much by the soundness of her project, but by her utter composure and confidence despite the odds stacked against her. Was this the same young nun whom he had known so well, who, as her companions related, had been too nervous even to light the candles before Mass as a novice? And yet she had radiated confidence. Father Henry recorded this historic visit with Mother Teresa in his diary:

> Today, 19th August, 1949, Mother Mary Teresa is leaving Saint Mary's, Entally, to work in the slums of Calcutta for the poor. For this very difficult task she places all of her confidence in the Immaculate Heart of Mary.

For this immensely difficult task, she had placed all of her confidence in the heart of Our Lady. How could someone as practical and down-to-earth, as realistic and unsentimental as Mother Teresa, declare that she was facing the daunting challenges of mission work on the streets of Calcutta simply by placing "all of her confidence" in Our Lady? And why specifically in her Immaculate Heart? Because Mother Teresa came to understand that Our Lady's heart — meaning her soul, her interiority, the grace she carried within — was not only a sacred space in which to dwell and hear the voice of the Crucified One, but was a gift that Our Lady was able to share. After praying that Our Lady would "*keep her in her heart,*" Mother Teresa asked that Our Lady "*lend her her heart*" that she might love her Lord and her neighbor in the way Mary did.

Mother Teresa's charism and spirituality is something entire and organic, and her intimate relationship with Our Lady is an integral part of it. I saw this in her over the years, as did so many of her Sisters and co-workers: that in facing whatever difficulties, great and small, she placed her entire confidence in Our Lady's presence and aid. If we wish to experience the closeness and power of God that was Mother Teresa's daily bread, we need first examine our relationship with Our Lady. Have we yet to give her our confidence? To place our worries, our weaknesses, our sinfulness, our struggles with prayer and spiritual life in Our Lady's hands? And if not, why not?

This is the first step. We won't get further in following Mother Teresa if we don't first take this one. This is what divides Mother Teresa and her holiness from the struggles and failures of so many who admire and seek to imitate her, even among those who are members of her own religious order. So many have the same love for the poor; they work night and day, they spend the same amount of time in prayer, but they don't have her relationship with Our Lady. Because of that, they don't share in the depth of her relationship with Jesus crucified.

'Lend Us Your Heart'

The second step is to ask Our Lady, as did Mother Teresa, to "lend us" her heart. What exactly does this mean? How can Our Lady lend us her heart? When Mother Teresa was asked this question, she would reply that this was not a mere pious sentiment, but a concrete, lived reality. A great mystic and theologian of the early centuries, St. Ephraim of Syria, once wrote, "May the spirit of Mary be in every soul to glorify the Lord." Our Lady's relationship with Christ her Son is not something she keeps for herself. It is for her children, and she is more than able to dispense such gifts abundantly.

It seems clear that some of the anointing the Father placed on Our Lady and on her role at Calvary he in turn placed upon Mother Teresa. Mother Teresa's mission made Our Lady's presence and role visible before our eyes, reminding us of what Our Lady had done at the foot of the Cross, of what she does eternally in the heavenly liturgy around the throne of the Lamb (see Rev 5:12), and of what she does invisibly here on earth.

> *I entrust you all to Our Lady, the Virgin Mother of God, whom Jesus on the Cross gave us to be our Mother also. May she give her heart, so beautiful, so pure, so immaculate, so full of love and humility.*[18]

Communion with Mary

Mother Teresa lived an intimate communion with the person and grace of Our Lady. Mary became the spiritual atmosphere in which Mother Teresa lived and worked, prayed and loved. This hidden but powerful interior union made of Mother Teresa a kind of extension of Our Lady's presence. Many of Mother Teresa's Sisters and co-workers have commented on her relationship to Our Lady in similar terms, speaking of her as an embodiment of Our Lady in our midst.

Mother Teresa taught her followers that all are invited to share in this anointing and grace. All stand, like St. John, at the foot of the Cross of her Son, and all are called to entrust themselves to Mary, who stands mystically at their side. We give her our heart in consecration, that she might "lend us her heart," and prepare our soul for unimagined gifts of the Spirit.

Chapter Five

Living Our Lady's Spirit

---◦---

The Spirit of the Society

In the ensuing months and years after her experience on the train, a new response of grace began to well up in Mother Teresa, which she recognized as coming entirely from Our Lady. Eventually, she was able to describe this new grace in writing, to better define the concrete manner in which Our Lady was keeping her promise to lend her the grace of her heart. Ever practical, she wanted not only to insist on the importance of Our Lady for her Sisters and followers, but to explain how Our Lady supplied for their spiritual inadequacies and brought them to holiness and intimacy with God. This she categorized in what she called the "Spirit of the Missionaries of Charity Society," and she formulated it in three states of soul: (1) loving trust, (2) total surrender, and (3) cheerfulness, or cheerful giving. She saw this threefold spirit as so essential that she later included it in the Constitutions of the Society.[19] She constantly presented the Spirit of the Society as an extension of and participation in Our Lady's spirit:

> If we stand with Our Lady, she will give us her spirit of loving trust, total surrender and cheerfulness.[20]

> Lent is once again with us, a precious time when Jesus, through His Church, asks us to keep our minds and hearts fixed on His deep longing for our loving

trust in His love, expressed by our total surrender to His loving will, so as to be able to share His joy of being one with the Father.[21]

The gospel account of the Annunciation and Visitation (see Lk 1:26-56) shows this triple response modeled by Our Lady. We see Mary's *trust* in accepting the word of the angel, as attested by Elizabeth: "Blessed is she who believed [trusted] that there would be a fulfillment of what was spoken to her from the Lord" (Lk 1:45 — RSV). We see her *surrender* before the unknown future held in God's plan: "Let it be to me according to your word" (Lk 1:38 — RSV). And we see her *cheerful gift* in the joy with which she answers God's call: "My spirit rejoices in God my Savior" (Lk 1:47 — RSV). Later, we see Our Lady communicating that joy to others: "Behold, when the voice of your greeting came to my ears, the child in my womb leaped for joy" (Lk 1:44 — RSV).

He has given us Our Lady's spirit to be the Spirit of our Society . . . Loving Trust and Total Surrender made Our Lady say "Yes" to the message of the angel, and Cheerfulness made her to run in haste to serve her cousin Elizabeth. That is so much our life — saying, "Yes" to Jesus and running in haste to serve Him in the poorest of the poor. Let us keep close to Our Lady and she will make that same spirit grow in each one of us.[22]

The Dynamics of Love

The Spirit of the Society — trust, surrender, and joyful giving — are the natural response to being loved totally and freely. These are not three separate virtues, but rather a single threefold response to meeting God's "infinite longing to love and be loved," communicated especially in Jesus crucified.

> The Spirit [of] our Society — loving trust, total surrender, and cheerfulness — was born of Mother [Teresa's] experience of the Thirst of Jesus.[23]

Can we not find a parallel to this in our own experience? Take someone who has had a happy childhood surrounded by the love of his parents. Ask him to describe his childhood and he will say that first of all he felt loved. How did he respond to that love? Without much thought he found himself spontaneously trusting his parents and their care for him. If they brought him somewhere or did something that he was too young to understand, he went along without question or complaint. He surrendered to what they did without a thought. Finally, he remembers that his childhood was full of joy, a joy that he could not help sharing with his family and friends. This is the same dynamic we see at work in the Spirit of the Society, the same response Mother found within her, a result of her experience of Jesus' thirst to love her.

Our Lady's Magnificat

It has recently been revealed that, like so many other great saints, Mother Teresa experienced a painful and prolonged "dark night of the soul." In the midst of her pain, she was able to find God through her faith; not simply believing that God existed, but having a total reliance on God without insisting to see or to understand. This kind of unwavering faith, lived so well in Mother Teresa, finds its model in Our Lady. What did Our Lady do during the moments of darkness in her life? She trusted. She asked no questions, nor did she complain. She did not run away. She accepted the darkness, and never pulled back from the sword that was piercing her heart. She believed in spite of human appearances:

> At the foot of the Cross, Our Lady saw only pain and suffering — and when they closed the tomb, she could not even see the Body of Jesus. But it was then that Our Lady's faith, her Loving Trust and Total Surrender were greatest. We know that before, in Nazareth, Jesus could not work any miracles because they had no faith. Now, to work His greatest miracle — the Resurrection — He asks the greatest faith from His own Mother. And because she belonged completely to God in Loving Trust and Total Surrender, He could bring to us the joy of the Resurrection, and Mary would be the Cause of our Joy.[24]

Our Lady listened to one voice, God's voice, instead of the thousand others, voices that spoke of terrible dangers, of impossible situations, of misunderstandings, persecution, rejection, injustice, and unspeakable pain that awaited Jesus in his Passion. She heard but one voice. In this she is not only our mother but our model. She wants to give birth to this same spirit of trust and surrender in us, even as she did for Mother Teresa. Mary's humility at not insisting to know and understand gave her tremendous freedom, and gave God the freedom to use her.

Our Lady's *Magnificat*, perhaps the most complete reflection of her spirit, is also a canticle to the spirit of Mother Teresa's Society, and provides a pattern for our own attitudes of soul. The power of the *Magnificat* lies in Our Lady's awareness of being so immensely loved by God, so specially chosen. She does not believe she deserves this. She knew that God had loved her in her lowliness (see Lk 1:48). This experience of love leads Our Lady to spontaneous trust and praise and frees her from self-concern. But in this poetic psalm, Our Lady sings of God's love not only for her, but for all. The majority of the *Magnificat* exults in what God has done for Israel and for all humanity from the dawning of time. This joy, based in trust and surrender, will follow Our Lady all the way to Calvary, carry her through her Son's burial, and bring her steadfast to Easter Sunday.

The surest mark of a believing Christian is the freedom to praise, the freedom to sing one's own *Magnificat*. Our Lady accompanies us in this process, and even where there is necessary loss or salutary pain, she turns all to joy. She frees our spirit to write our own *Magnificat* with the lines of our lives, frees us from complaint to live in praise. She lends us her heart that we might live her spirit. Just as Mother Teresa radiated joy in the midst of pain, so too we can radiate the joy of Our Lady's spirit to all with whom we come in contact. May the title Mother Teresa gave to Our Lady, the fruit of her constant experience in her company, become our experience as well: Immaculate Heart of Mary, Cause of our Joy, lend us your heart.

Chapter Six

In Silent Prayer with Mary

---◦---

The Silence of the Heart

The first thing that people noticed in Mother Teresa when she came to prayer was that she immediately went to the depths of her being. Her most repeated quotation on prayer was "*In the silence of the heart God speaks.*"

In the heart, not the head.

Mother Teresa is ever teaching what Our Lady modeled for us: that we cannot pray satisfactorily by staying on the surface of our soul. This leaves us like a paper cup on the surface of the sea, buffeted by the waves and wind of distraction. If instead we go deeper, like a diver seeking precious pearls, we will find peace and treasure. Pearls do not float on the surface. We can spend all day in the water, just as we can spend all day in prayer, and go home with nothing, unless we pierce the depths. The seat and center of our waking consciousness is normally at the "head" level. This is where our five senses are, and where we interact with the world. But this is not the place of encounter with God. We need to pass to the level of the heart. The heart, in Mother Teresa's understanding of Our Lady and her interior life, represents the place of inner quiet, not feelings or sentimentality but rather inner depth, the silent place where God speaks.

As we come to this deeper place of the heart, we open ourselves to the activity of the Holy Spirit. If we allow him to do his work in silence, we will perceive that something is happening at a deep level of our being. We begin to realize that only God can love us this way. No mere human can give us this much love, nor place that love so deeply in our being.

The more we discover the magnitude and abundance of God's gifts, the more we will find in ourselves what Mother Teresa experienced in Our Lady. We begin to expect good things from God. We expect him to bless us in a special way, today. We find ourselves looking forward to each day, like a child on Christmas Eve. What surprise of love has the Father prepared for me today? What gifts has he prepared for my family? We enter into a state of faith. This was the attitude and life breath of Our Lady. As Jesus assures us in the gospel, it will be done to us according to our faith. Perhaps we least expect the miracles of Jesus because we have become too familiar with him or with what we think we know of him. We tie the hands of God with our lack of faith. We expect no miracles, so none occur.

Take, Lord, Receive

As we experience ourselves being filled with God's love and blessings, with the fruit of his constant self-emptying, we are moved to our own self-emptying and self-gift in return. This, too, begins in prayer. In this kind of prayer, it does not matter what we feel or what the conditions are for prayer; whether we're sick, tired, or have a headache. We are pouring the reality of ourselves out at the feet of the Lord.

Our Lady taught Mother Teresa that even pain could become a place of prayer. What seems to the world a lack of God's presence becomes a place of meeting. As Job sat in the ashes, so we can sit in our pain before the crucified Lord. Instead of struggling with pain as a distraction to our prayer, we can integrate our suffering into our prayer. We can lift our pain up to the Lord on the Cross, and hold it there before him. We can be there in peace, even in darkness, with that part of us that says "Why, Lord?" If we remain there with the brokenness this represents in us, we give Jesus the opportunity to be our Savior, to be our Resurrection again in the present, to take this pain and this problem and make it a part of his own Passion, and the doorway to share his Resurrection.

Christ has the power to do this, if we give him permission. He will transform our suffering and raise it to the Father. Though the pain might remain, our anguish will turn to peace. There will be healing of bitterness, of resentment, and of despair. Jesus does not take away all our wounds, any more than the Father erased all of his wounds. Rather, he disinfects them and glorifies them. For Jesus, the Resurrection was not an emergency room where the Father took away all the signs of the Passion. Jesus rose with his wounds, wounds now transformed from darkness to light, dug into his hands in time and in pain and now become eternal fonts of light and blessing and glory.

Nor is the Resurrection Jesus' reward for having suffered. It is rather the unstoppable explosion of glory that pours forth from Love's triumph on the Cross. When the fullness of the Father's love was revealed and released in Jesus' death, its power entered first into Jesus' body in the Resurrection, and will one day fill and raise the whole world. The Lord will do with our wounds the same as he did with that unspeakable wound that pierced Our Lady's heart, so that we too may also rise with him.

Mother Teresa's Favorite Prayer — the Rosary

Mother Teresa's favorite and most frequent prayer as she practiced union with Our Lady was, without doubt, the Rosary.

The Rosary becomes true prayer of the heart when we pray it slowly and deeply, when we seek a deeper level of soul, staying at the level of the heart, wrapped in Our Lady, meditating with her the events of our salvation in Jesus her Son. The particular power of the Rosary as a means of grace, of entering into that sacred space so prized by Mother Teresa, has been underlined by Our Lady herself in virtually all of her apparitions around the world, not to mention her own words to Mother Teresa:

> *"Take care of them — they are mine. — Bring them to Jesus — carry Jesus to them. — Fear not. Teach them to say the Rosary — the family Rosary and all will be well. . . ."*[25]

Though it is often misunderstood, and therefore poorly prayed, the Rosary is indeed a form of contemplative prayer. Pope John Paul II wrote, in his apostolic letter on the Rosary:

> The Rosary, precisely because it starts with Mary's own experience, is an exquisitely contemplative prayer. Without this contemplative dimension, it would lose its meaning, as Pope Paul VI clearly pointed out: "Without contemplation, the Rosary is a body without a soul, and its recitation runs the risk of becoming a mechanical repetition of formulas, in violation of the admonition of Christ: 'In praying do not heap up empty phrases as the Gentiles do; for they think they will be heard for

their many words' (Mt 6:7). By its nature the recitation of the Rosary calls for a quiet rhythm and a lingering pace, helping the individual to meditate on the mysteries of the Lord's life as seen through the eyes of her who was closest to the Lord. In this way the unfathomable riches of these mysteries are disclosed" (apostolic exhortation *Marialis Cultus* [February 2, 1974], 47: AAS [1974], 156).[26]

Those who lived with Mother Teresa knew that she held a rosary in her hand constantly, in everything she did and everywhere she went. This was her way not only of holding Our Lady's hand, but of recalling and reliving her founding vision. This vision helps us to understand and, if we so desire, to follow this humble Nobel Prize winner who placed all her confidence in the heart of Mary, and who spent her life as she is surely now spending her eternity, in the Shadow of Our Lady.

Chapter Seven

Contemplatives in the Heart of the World

Mother Teresa insisted that she and her Sisters, and those who wished to live her charism, were called to be contemplatives in the heart of the world, contemplatives in the midst of action. But to do so, they had first to learn what it meant to be contemplatives.

St. Ignatius would say that contemplative prayer, "prayer of the heart," prayer of interior depth, involves going beyond formalities and set times. It is an ability to "seek and find God in all things." Seeking and finding God in all things was Mother Teresa's secret to ceaseless prayer, a secret she received from Our Lady who "treasured up all these things and pondered them in her heart" (Lk 2:19 — NIV).

Before finding the Lord Jesus in what Mother Teresa called the distressing disguise of suffering and failure, whether mine or those of my family and friends, we need first to be experts in the contemplative life, masters at finding God in the little details of life. God is in every reality. How else could Mother Teresa have served fifty years in the worst of conditions, unless she was tapping into something real and divine hidden under the surface? How could she have kept her peace and her joy in the face of so much human tragedy, without a deeper, larger vision? And from what source could she have drawn and nourished that vision of faith except in prayer with Our Lady? "*The fruit of prayer is faith*," Mother Teresa used to repeat to the crowds whenever she spoke in public. If we live only on the surface of things, we reject what we do not understand, what pains or costs or frustrates us. But God is there.

The Fruits of Deep Prayer

Mother Teresa's union of prayer with Our Lady produced not only insight, not only light in the darkness, but strength and heroic resilience. Once, when visiting her Sisters in Tanzania, the small plane carrying Mother Teresa went suddenly off course during landing, tearing through the crowd of well-wishers who had come to greet her. The propellers of the plane literally shredded two of her Sisters, who expired on the spot. Mother Teresa had to face the fact that, in some way, she had been the cause of their death. As she disembarked and surveyed the tragic scene, she was heard to say under her breath, "*God's will*..." Nothing more, nothing else. Only a life of deep prayer could produce that kind of deep faith.

Such faith comes from a heart well-trained in finding God in everything. This was the gift of Our Lady who, long before Mother Teresa, stood at another Calvary and said: "God's will." We may not be at that level, but we can begin to walk in that direction, to walk peacefully, prayerfully, through the contradictions of daily life. To live prayerfully in the company of Our Lady is the key.

If we have but "faith as small as a mustard seed" (Mt 17:20 — NIV), God will move mountains for us in his determination to bless us. We will see for ourselves what Our Lady and Mother Teresa knew intimately, that "in all things God works for the good" (Rom 8:28 — NIV). This is true for all those who love God, always. But to have that kind of vision of faith, we need deep prayer, not just a perfunctory Mass on Sunday or a few hasty prayers before bed. When we do pray, before we open our minds or lips, we need to open our heart. Our Lady teaches us to pray before we pray, to yearn for him who yearns for us before we ever approach him.

St. Ignatius expressed this principle in two famous meditations from his Spiritual Exercises that would mold the prayer life of a young Mother Teresa. As a girl in her home parish in Skopje, Macedonia, and later as a nun of the Loreto order, she was formed in the spirituality of St. Ignatius. In his Exercises, Ignatius shows how God uses all created things to bless us and to draw us to himself. Everything in our life is woven into the Father's perfect plan. Ignatius' closing prayer exercise, the Contemplation to Attain Love, which Mother Teresa would have meditated on every year during her annual retreat, leads us not just to understand God's love for us, but to fill ourselves with divine love, at a deeper and deeper level, so as to love him and others with the very love we receive.

St. Ignatius shows us that love by its nature gives of itself. God communicates himself in giving his gifts. Everything God does in our life fills us with him, if we have but eyes to see. Once we have realized this through prayer, we can genuinely help others in their moments of pain and crisis. People need more than our sympathy; they need the light of awareness of God's presence with them. Our faith, developed in prayer, can supply whatever may be their lack in their struggle with faith. Just as Mother Teresa communicated her faith to thousands of those who were struggling on the streets of Calcutta, or drawing their last breath in her Home for the Dying next to Kali Temple, or listening to her speak in Europe and America, so can we share the light we have received. A single flame can set a forest ablaze, and a single word of light, a word spoken in faith and born of prayer, can spread that same light to a soul plunged in darkness and doubt.

The Daily Examen

St. Ignatius weaves all these principles into a simple daily exercise called the Examen. This is more than just an examination of conscience. It is a prayerful examination of what God has been doing and giving me this day. We go back to recover the gifts and graces overlooked yet still active in the events of the day. Like pieces in a grand mosaic, all of God's graces are important. The Father wishes his children to be equipped with the full complement of grace and love he has prepared for them day by day. The Examen is a means that Mother Teresa used to enter into Our Lady's practice of "pondering" the great and small doings of God on a daily basis.

One practical way of doing the Examen is to prayerfully consider, before retiring, five gifts or blessings we have received during that day. Doing this daily, we become more aware of God's gifts, and of God himself as a giver of gifts, rather than only as a judge. We begin to see his goodness where before we saw only his supposed absence. Like Mother Teresa, we can make this Examen with Our Lady, who will help us see, through her eyes, the plan and presence of God all around us. Our Lady helps us to see and experience the constant love of God. The more we see with our eyes, the more we can experience with our heart. And the more we experience with our heart, the more we become capable of seeing with our eyes on the next occasion.

From here we can move to the second part of the Examen, in which we discover five moments when we were invited to give of ourselves, five occasions in which grace was inviting us to generosity. We then thank God where we have succeeded, and ask for healing and forgiveness where we struggled and failed. This practice helps us to refocus our thirst for God, the only one who can truly satisfy us. God's thirst for us is only repaid by our thirst for him.

As we take a few moments of time to "pray before praying," to seek God and the anointing of his presence upon all things, we move deeper into that presence and then rest there, stay there, learn to live there. St. Ignatius recommends meditating upon a passage of Scripture until we feel some interior movement, what he calls "consolation" in the sense of a movement of grace. We wait to be touched. Once we experience that touch of grace, we stay there as long as it lasts. The same is true with prayer in general. We start our prayer waiting for some sense of God. Once we find it, we stay there. Sometimes it will seem more superficial, sometimes it will go very deep. It is best not to start reciting formal prayers until we know the depth to which the Lord wishes to take us.

This is a quiet process; it is as if we were in a room full of closed and locked doors in the dark, feeling our way, touching each door gently to see if it opens, then entering through one door into the Presence. Once again, Our Lady is a great help in this. She is an unparalleled aid in entering this inner quiet. Like Mother Teresa in her vision, we allow ourselves to be wrapped in Our Lady's presence before we approach the mystery of God. With her, we go deeper into the words of her Son, which she pondered so long and so well.

We can do something similar during the day, outside of times of prayer. We wait on the anointing with Our

Lady, and as soon as we perceive something of God's presence, we rest in it, whether we encounter that presence while driving the car, doing the accounting, or walking down the street. We begin to be more aware of the anointing of God on everything; it becomes habitual.

At the Crosses of Life

Our Lady helps us, as Mother Teresa found in her third vision, to become contemplatives at the foot of the Cross. Like Mother Teresa, we too come to understand that Jesus' cry of thirst from the Cross is a creative Divine Word, a word of power by which he draws us to himself. By his word of thirst, of yearning, God in Jesus is drawing us to himself, and that means also to his Cross. This he will do, as long as we stay near Our Lady, despite our fears, our laziness, our attachments. At times we can even feel ourselves being drawn, though we often don't know how to respond. Standing with Our Lady, we experience most clearly the draw of Christ and his Cross. We also best understand its opposite, the draw toward our false thirsts: our own will, our own ease, our self-glorification. Our Lady is the place where all of that falsehood can be named and purified with a minimum of effort and pain. Over time, as we continue to live with her in trust and docility, we experience ourselves being washed clean. Our soul, like a dry and thirsty sponge, begins absorbing the overflowing of the spirit coming from Our Lady's interior life, as Elizabeth caught Mary's inner spirit at her Visitation.

Many of us, from the time we were small, have known how to pray to Our Lady. The difference here is that Mother Teresa is inviting us to an ongoing relationship with Mary:

Let us not think that we are working along with her
if we only say a few prayers in her honor. We must live
habitually with her. . . .[27]

In the light of Mary's presence everything becomes different, and we see in a new way the beauty of God's presence in us and around us.

Contemplatives in the World

How then are we to become contemplatives, to pray more deeply? Many of us experienced that our early fervor in prayer dwindled eventually into dryness, and that we struggled with distraction. This is what the tradition of the Church has called the Night of the Senses, something that Mother Teresa lived very acutely, in which we no longer feel the anointing of grace with our emotional apparatus. When this night comes, we often either stop praying or, if we continue praying, do so only superficially. This breeds dissatisfaction with our prayer life, and we remain frustrated in our thirst for God. What is actually happening when there is dryness at the emotional level of the soul, a dryness Mother Teresa knew all too well? As the great Spanish mystic St. John of the Cross tells us, the anointing has not disappeared; it has only moved. That living font of grace has not been withdrawn; it has gone deeper, beyond the senses.

Traditionally, two responses to this struggle have given birth to two different spiritualities. The first was called *fuga mundi*, or "flight from the world." This response rested on the conviction that one must flee the noise of the world if one is to find God. In order to pray, we need to remove ourselves, as far as possible, from all distractions. According to the second kind of spirituality represented by both St. Ignatius and Mother Teresa, we choose to find God in all things, even to the point of finding God in the worst things, in pain and in poverty, in the Cross. What seemed darkness becomes light. What seemed defeat, for Jesus in his Passion or for us in our sufferings, becomes victory.

Jesus told Mother Teresa that her interior life would be her only support in this difficult mission she was undertaking. The importance of the daily Examen is found here: it made her, and can make us, into "active contemplatives." It allowed Mother Teresa to see and touch Jesus in the poor. Otherwise, the poor are no longer Christ, but only a cause.

Mother Teresa had a marked awareness of God's interventions in everything. This awareness filled her with a spirit of wonder. It became a source of joy for her and gave her energy. The first time I had the opportunity to travel with Mother Teresa, I asked her, "What is it like, living what you live there in Calcutta?" She spent the rest of the flight relating example after example of how God takes care of his children. It took me many years to understand that she was trying to teach me to find God all around me, even in the worst of places. To her eyes, miracles were everywhere. God had not become deaf or crippled; he was still powerfully at work in all things.

Remembering at least five blessings every day, seeing with eyes of faith the presence and goodness of God in everything, we begin to understand the heart of God. We begin to be like Mother Teresa: full of wonder, spontaneously full of joy and energy, because of the realization that everything is gift; all is grace.

Chapter Eight

Consecration to Our Lady

————◦◦————

Mother Teresa's practical way to live the intimacy and dependency on Our Lady, symbolized in her three visions, was through the practice of Marian entrustment, or "consecration." This was the means by which she and her followers would take Our Lady into their hearts:

> She [Mary] as first Missionary of Charity went in haste to help Jesus sanctify John — and so it will be with you and me if we only love her unconditionally and trust her fully. The more we abandon ourselves to her totally and without reserve, the greater will be the number of great saints in our Society — for nothing is impossible for those whose Mother she is. Often during the day, let us raise our heart to her and ask her how she would do this or that now if she was in our place — and above all how to love God as she loved him, that we too may love him with her heart.[28]

John Paul II wrote that consecration to Our Lady produces "a life of intense communion and familiarity with the Blessed Virgin, as a 'new way' of living for God."[29] We hand over everything we have and are — past, present, and future — so that she might continue through us her mission on earth:

> How much we need Mary to teach us what it means to satiate God's thirsting Love for us which Jesus came to reveal to us — She did it so beautifully. Yes, Mary

allowed God to take possession of her life by Her
purity, Her humility and Her faithful love. . . . It is
in doing so that, like Mary our Mother, we will allow
God to take full possession of our whole being — and
through us God will be able to reach out His thirst-
ing love to all we come in contact with, especially the
poor people He entrusts to us.[30]

While Our Lady is mother of all, Mother Teresa realized that the mission entrusted to her and to her followers (amongst whom are included the many lay people
around the world who seek to live her spirit in their own
surroundings) made them Mary's possession in a particular way. She recognized that the Congregation she
founded belonged entirely to Our Lady. That is why she
taught her Sisters to pray:

"Immaculate Heart of Mary, Cause of our Joy, bless
your own Missionaries of Charity. Help us to do all
the good we can. Keep us in your most pure Heart, so
that we may please Jesus through you, in you, and
with you."[31]

Personal Covenant

Mother Teresa's sense of the demands and the depths to
which she was invited in her relationship with God, with
Our Lady, and with the poor led her to a radicality and
generosity that made her the saint she became. While not
sentimental, Mother Teresa was nonetheless extraordinar-
ily loving. She spoke of clinging to Jesus, and she used
the most ardent spousal language. She employed an
equally ardent tone, that of a child who gives all her heart
to her mother, in referring to the gift of self to Our Lady:

Cling to Our Lady.[32]

The way that we "cling to Our Lady," in Mother Teresa's mind, is by establishing a personal covenant of life with her. This was the kind of covenant Jesus himself established between his mother and St. John on Calvary, when he said to John, "She will be your Mother, and you will be her son" (cf. Jn 19:26-27). Our covenant relationship with Our Lady is a kind of consecration by which we entrust ourselves and our whole lives entirely to her, and become thereby "particularly her own." Consecration to Our Lady is not a matter of words; it is rather a covenant of life shared with her in the service of her Son.

The first Missionary of Charity Sisters clearly understood from the beginning the importance Mother Teresa ascribed to their entrusting all to Our Lady. They remember that Mother Teresa's way was very, very simple; that "she always, always, told us to go to our mother — Our Lady — and cling to her like a little child. This I learnt from Mother from the time I joined."[33]

> [Mother Teresa] encouraged us to make the Total Consecration to Our Lady with 30-days preparation according to St. Louis de Montfort. We do that very faithfully and renew our total consecration to Our Lady every year. . . . Mother taught us that when we go to Our Lady with childlike confidence, everything becomes easy. Mother always led us to Our Lady and continually gave Our Lady as an example for everything.[34]

Mother Teresa understood that it was only when Jesus saw such a covenant established in our hearts that he would entrust to us the secrets of his longing love. The two flow from each other, just as the two passages that record them follow in direct succession: "Behold, your mother" and "I thirst" (Jn 19:27, 28 — RSV). To live in a covenant relationship with her means not only that, like St. John, we "take her unto our own" (cf. Jn 19:27) as a presence in our daily lives, but that we give her authority over ourselves and all that belongs to us.

Our consecration can be summarized in this way: it is the resolution to remain always in her heart, carefree, without attachments or worries, in constant prayer of heart and docility of will:

> *Let us all together consecrate our lives totally to Her . . . so that through Her guidance & help each of us [may] become the true Spouse of Jesus Crucified, a true M[issionary] of C[harity].*[35]

Below are eight essential components necessary to the kind of authentic and fruitful consecration that Mother Teresa encouraged.

1. TOTAL CONFIDENCE in Mary, and in her role and power in our life, with the conviction that together we can and will fulfill our vocation and reach the union with God to which we are called.

2. PRESENCE: Faith in the reality and constancy of Mary's presence in our daily life; knowing that she is always with us, that she always hears us, and that her loving gaze ever penetrates our soul.

3. ABSOLUTE TRUST in her, in all that she is doing in our life in the present moment, and in all that concerns our future, expecting everything from her at all times and in every situation, knowing that all is being arranged by her for our good.

4. ABANDONMENT: The living out of our trust; the act of free cooperation with Our Lady's activity in our life;

abandonment both in the specific circumstances we are living, and as a general attitude of soul, allowing ourselves to be led by her, giving to her all attachments, worries, expectations, and desires, and offering her the gift of interior and exterior docility.

5. SELF-GIFT: Giving ourselves in her service, to carry out her plan and to aid in the accomplishment of her mission; giving to the Lord through her all we have and are, our entire self and all that concerns us.

6. ENTERING HER HEART: Living in the temple of her interior being, in spiritual communion and incessant prayer with her; to dwell with her in the presence of the Trinity; to listen to her and learn from her; to know that our soul will be transformed into the image of Jesus by the Spirit at work within her.

7. SHARING HER PRAYER: Meditating on the Word of God together with her, listening to Jesus.

8. SHARING HER MISSION: Living at the foot of the Cross with her; bringing Jesus with her to the lost, the least, and the last; to be the channel of her presence and activity, totally at her disposal for the service of Jesus in those God has placed in our life; to console her and share in her sorrow over the suffering of her Son and his Mystical Body.

To the extent that we are in her and of her, we will be in and of Christ the Lord; to the extent that she is in us, living and praying, serving and consoling, channeling the living waters of the Spirit of Love, we will be able to live the same graces as Mother Teresa lived, in the Calcutta of our own lives:

With Mary, we make more progress in the love of Jesus in one month than we make in years while liv-

ing less united to this good Mother (citing de Mont-fort).[36]

To summarize the spirit of our lived consecration, we can take an idea from St. Margaret Mary Alacoque. When, after her initial revelations concerning devotion to the Sacred Heart of Jesus (with the same biblical meaning of heart that Mother Teresa understood so well), she couldn't understand what Jesus meant by consecrating herself to him, Jesus gave her a simple yet beautiful formula: "You think of me; I will be the one to think of you. You look to my needs and those of your neighbor; I will look to yours." This simple arrangement can be applied to our consecration to Our Lady as well. It is very demanding, but very liberating. We see it in the *Nican Mopohua* of Juan Diego; we see it in Mother Teresa and her *Spirit of the Society*.

Living Our Covenant

The basic thrust of Marian consecration involves placing everything in her hands and in her heart, and sharing our life with her so that she can share her life with us.

We must . . . abandon ourselves completely into her hands.[37]

Our covenant with Our Lady is based on her one "great commandment" to us: "Do whatever he tells you" (Jn 2:5 — RSV). Once again it is Our Lady who initiates this entire process. She sees and knows our need; she intercedes for the graces that we lack and prepares us to receive them. Our covenant with Our Lady needs to take concrete form as well as mental and spiritual assent. The Holy Spirit will guide us in choosing the terms of our personal covenant in complete freedom, but on the next page are a few suggestions and principles for drafting and preparing to live such a covenant.

The Daily Encounter

Our covenant requires one essential: We need to spend personal time each day with Our Lady. This means dedicating some moments, no matter how brief, to conscious contact with her. Only by dedicating such times to encounter her in spirit will she increasingly become a concrete presence in our life. It was Mother Teresa's daily encounter with Our Lady that strengthened and equipped her for her work among the poorest, and for the countless challenges she faced at every turn. The same is true for us. A personal daily encounter with Our Lady is not something extra, peripheral, or marginal. From Mother Teresa's experience we can see that it is both central and essential. The encounter with Our Lady lets us live beyond our limitations, wrapped in her presence and sharing her spirit and her heart. Without this daily encounter, we will never learn to listen to her, whispering her wisdom and infusing her light in the depths of our souls. Without opening to her, there will be no entrustment of self, no surrender to her and through her to God. Without the support of her *Fiat*, our good-willed but fragile assent to the Lord will too often waver, and she will not be able to do what only she can do in our lives.

The length of time given to our visits with Our Lady is not as important as their frequency and constancy. Our encounter with her leads to an encounter with God, which we could not have reached on our own. Our encounter with her is not opposed to or distracting from our encounter with God. The lived experience of those closest

Marian Covenant

"Moved by an ardent desire to live in the closest union with you possible in this life, so as to more surely and fully arrive at union with your Son; I hereby pledge to live the spirit and terms of the following Covenant of Consecration as faithfully and generously as I am able."

Her Duties	My Duties
1. To give of her spirit and heart.	1. Total gift of all I have and am.
2. To possess, protect, and transform me.	2. Total dependence on her.
3. To inspire, guide, and enlighten me.	3. Responsiveness to her spirit.
4. To share her experience of prayer and praise.	4. Faithfulness to prayer.
5. Responsibility for my sanctification.	5. Trust in her intercession.
6. Responsibility for all that befalls me.	6. Accept all as coming from her.
7. To share with me her virtues.	7. Imitate her spirit.
8. To provide for my spiritual and material needs.	8. Constant recourse to her.
9. Union with her heart.	9. Remembrance of her presence.
10. To purify me and my actions.	10. Purity of intention; self-denial.
11. Right to dispose of me, of my prayers and intercessions and graces.	11. Right to avail myself of her and energies for the sake of the kingdom.
12. Total freedom in and around me, as she pleases in all things.	12. Right to enter into her heart, to share her interior life.

to God over two millennia tells us, as does the experience of the contemporary and non-sentimental Mother Teresa, that our encounter with Our Lady leads to and enhances our encounter with God.

In Conclusion

We come back to the place where we began, with Mother Teresa's vision at the outset of her new life, surrounded by the poor, close to Mary before the Cross of Christ. We come back to this new way of living and of loving God that would change her and thousands of others around the globe, rich and poor alike. Everything is there: Our Lady enfolding Mother Teresa as she desires to enfold us, in her presence and love, in order to bring us to the Cross of Jesus, hidden in the Eucharist and in the poor, to bring light where the world sees only darkness. Our Lady invites us to do what she has done: to bring everything, our pain and hopes, to the Cross, so that Jesus can lift the cup of our lives to the Father, and transform all into seeds of Resurrection.

The Biblical Foundations of Mother Teresa's Relationship with Mary

---◆---

The Role of the Blessed Mother

To Our Lady has been entrusted the entire work of preparing the New Israel for the "new wine" of God's love. Our Lady's role in the revelation of God's thirst for us began already at her conception as "full of grace" (Lk 1:28 — RSV). In her fullness of grace, she became the perfect mirror and vessel of the Trinity's desire to love and be loved by us. In her Annunciation, and for the nine months that she carried the Son of God within her, she came to experience as no other the depth of God's yearning to be with us. In giving Jesus birth, she brought God's love into the world. After his birth, what a longing and sense of responsibility she must have felt to care in every way for him who was the embodiment of the Father's immeasurable love. Can we not imagine that, in their thirty years of intimacy, Jesus would have opened his heart to her and spoken of the Father's longing which he had come to reveal? At Cana, as Jesus made his first appearance with his disciples, she would beg for this "new wine" of revelation. On Calvary, she was the first to hear and open her soul to his cry of thirst. It was on Calvary that she became the "woman" of Genesis, the New Eve, "mother of all the living" (Gen 3:20 — NAB). Disciple, "behold your mother!" (Jn 19:27 — RSV).

Our Lady's role in aiding and preparing the disciples continued, and continues, well beyond Calvary. We can picture her relating the great events of Calvary to the early disciples, gathered around her in prayer. She would be the one to prepare them after the Ascension for the gift of the "living waters" (Jer 2:13; cf. Jn 4:10 — RSV) to be poured out at Pentecost. We can see her sharing with John at Ephesus her understanding of the words they heard on Calvary, and the fire and urgency those words had impressed on her soul, perhaps even urging him to write them down for the Church.

After her Assumption, Our Lady's role was magnified immeasurably. As Jesus had ascended to the Father's right hand, living ever to intercede for us (cf. Heb 7:25), so Our Lady has joined him there, in fulfillment of his prayer: "Father, I want those you have given me to be with me where I am, and to see my glory, the glory you have given me because you loved me before the creation of the world" (Jn 17:24 — NIV). From there, as before, she would continue to intercede for the outpouring of his love on the Church and the world. As Jesus at his Ascension was given all power and authority in heaven and on earth (cf. Mt 28:18), so too Our Lady in the glory of her Coronation would receive a share in his power and authority over the whole of humanity, entrusted to her now as children.

It is Mary's role and her dignity to bring together the yearning of God and man, as she did first of all in her womb, as she did for John on Calvary, as she did for the disciples at Pentecost, as she did for Mother Teresa and Juan Diego, and as she will for each of us. She is the wedding place of God and man, the biblical "enclosed garden" (Song 4:12 — NAB), the new Eden to welcome and shelter our meeting with God.

Mother Teresa would extend, two thousand years later, Our Lady's mission in time and space. She would constantly beg of Our Lady, in her own name and in the name of her Sisters and co-workers, "*Lend us your heart.*" What might this mean? Whether Mother Teresa realized it or not, this request has biblical roots going back to the prophet Elijah. Our Lady's heart is still hers, but in God's plan it is also to be ours. The prayer, "*Lend us your heart,*" is not unlike Elisha's prayer as he begs the departing Elijah to lend him a "double portion" of his spirit (2 Kgs 2:9 — NAB). Mother Teresa is asking of Our Lady a double portion of her spirit, of her interior grace, her "heart," as she begins her new mission, carrying on the sacred task begun by Mary at the foot of the Cross. Mother Teresa's mission made Our Lady's presence and role visible before our eyes.

Our Lady and the Spirit

How is it possible for Our Lady to "lend us her heart"? The answer lies in Mary's privileged relationship to the Holy Spirit, in her Immaculate Conception. This mystery, with its many benefits, was intended for all of God's children, as sung by the Fathers of the Church from the earliest centuries:

> Today humanity, in all the radiance of [Our Lady's] immaculate nobility, receives its ancient beauty. The shame of sin had darkened the splendor and attraction of human nature; but when the Mother of the Fair One . . . is born, this nature

regains in her person its ancient privileges and is fashioned according to a perfect model truly worthy of God. . . . The reform of our nature begins today, and the aged world, subjected to a wholly divine transformation, receives the first fruits of the second creation.[38]

The Church tells us that Our Lady's Immaculate Conception was in view of her becoming the mother of the Son of God, the God-bearer, gilded with the Holy Spirit, as the ancient Ark of the Covenant was gilded with precious gold. St. Luke draws a stunning parallel between the episode of the Ark of the Covenant coming to David (see 2 Sam 6:2) and the New Ark that is Our Lady coming to Elizabeth (see Lk 1:39-40). As King David, the leader of Israel, dances for joy before the Ark (see 2 Sam 6:16), the unborn John the Baptist, who will lead Israel to the Messiah, leaps for joy before the Ark of Our Lady (see Lk 1:41). As David wonders how it is that the Ark of the Lord should come to him (see 2 Sam 6:9), Elizabeth marvels how it is that the mother of her Lord should come to her (see Lk 1:43). As the Ark stayed with David for three months (see 2 Sam 6:11), so Our Lady stayed three months with Elizabeth (see Lk 1:56).

In the Book of Revelation, we see this parallel celebrated again, this time in heaven. St John describes his vision: The heavens were opened, and in God's temple could be seen the Ark of the Covenant (see Rev 11:19). John immediately goes on in the next verse to describe a "woman clothed with the sun" (Rev 12:1 — RSV), as if to equate the two, as if he were presenting Our Lady as the true, new Ark, clothed in glory, even as Moses had presented the ancient Ark to Israel and described its glory (see Ex 25:10).

As Ark of the New Covenant, Our Lady not only has given us the One she carried in her womb; her presence remains forever a graced place of encounter between us and her Son. In the Old Testament, the Ark provided a sacred space where men could draw close to God, where grace flowed most freely, and where human foibles seemed somehow supplied for. It was a meeting place where man could contemplate the glory of God, where the cloud of glory bent down to touch the earth. Our Lady brings with her a sacred atmosphere filled with God's presence, offering a refuge that purifies and prepares us for the encounter with God. This was why Mother Teresa constantly asked Our Lady to keep her in her heart, to keep her within that sacred space, still pregnant with divinity.

I have twice had the privilege of entering the small room where the image of Our Lady of Guadalupe is kept. One side of the room is made of glass, through which the image is exposed for viewing. Once a month, at night, in order to clean the protective bullet-proof crystal, the image of Our Lady is swung on its hinges away from the glass. Certain people (such as writers, scholars, and scientists from NASA) have been given permission to examine the sacred image up close at such times, without the filter of thick leaded glass.

On that particular night, we were each given three minutes. As soon as I entered, I felt the overwhelming presence of Our Lady, a presence I can only name by what the Israelites called *kabod*, the weight of God's glory. My head dropped to the ground. After absorbing this living sense of God's glory that Our Lady was conveying through her invisible presence there, I told myself: "You only have three minutes; you had better look at her."

I understood for the first time the connection between God's glory and the temple, his dwelling place. I understood also that Our Lady is the meeting tent. She is the true temple.

For this reason, according to tradition, Our Lady as a child entered the temple, in order to be formed by the temple to *become* the temple, to resume in herself the mystery of God's presence in the history of his people, Israel, his chosen dwelling place among the nations. As the Fathers of the Church have affirmed, Mary *is* the mystery of the Church. In her, the Church is prefigured, contained, and brought to fulfillment. She is God's true Israel. All that God wanted to accomplish is realized, fulfilled, and perfected in Our Lady.

Our Lady Shares Her Gift

Our Lady is, in the language of tradition, "Spouse of the Holy Spirit." And yet, as St. Maximilian Kolbe and Pope John Paul II observed, to say "spouse," though it is the deepest of human relationships, is still far from describing the degree of union between Our Lady and the Holy Spirit. Pope John Paul, in his apostolic letter on the Rosary, defines Our Lady as the "Sanctuary of the Holy Spirit,"[39] precisely in referring to the Visitation. This union between Our Lady and the Holy Spirit is something for which we have no analogy. Here on this holy ground, the language of human experience fails us. Language can only point beyond what we can fathom, toward the full gift of Our Lady.

But Our Lady's relationship with the Holy Spirit is not something she keeps for herself. It is entirely for her children, and as Scripture shows us, she is more than able to dispense these gifts abundantly.

Let us return to Luke's account of the Visitation (see Lk 1:39-56). Elizabeth has conceived in her old age, and is to give birth to a son who will be the forerunner of the Messiah. Even though she has miraculously conceived, she is still in need of help. She has been feeling the weight of her own fragility for some months already when Mary unexpectedly arrives at her door, calling out Elizabeth's name. Elizabeth hears Mary's voice, and she discovers a spiritual revolution taking place within her:

> Elizabeth was filled with the Holy Spirit. In a loud voice she exclaimed: "Blessed are you among women, and blessed is the child you will bear! But why am I so favored, that the mother of my Lord should come to me? As soon as the sound of your greeting reached my ears, the baby in my womb leaped for joy." (Lk 1:41-44 — NIV)

What does this tell us? First of all, that there is an extraordinary anointing of the Holy Spirit on Our Lady's person, even on her voice. What Elizabeth discovered, and Mother Teresa after her, is that this anointing on Our Lady's presence is transmitted even when it is not sought or consciously attended to. For Our Lady's presence to be effective in our lives, even as for Mother Teresa or Elizabeth or the saints, she needs only to be welcomed and wanted, whether or not we are consistently conscious of her presence.

The Visitation demonstrates Our Lady's role not only in the life of Elizabeth, and of Mother Teresa, but of every disciple. At Mary's approach, Elizabeth is filled with the Holy Spirit. Not because she lacked the Holy Spirit until then: the Spirit was already working miraculously in her life in the conception of John. But with the coming of

Our Lady, there was a new and fuller outpouring of the Spirit, giving Elizabeth new energy and new hope for her task. The unborn life within her and her responsibility for it, a burden and source of worry until now, has suddenly become full of joy. What had caused her fatigue is now giving energy. *The child in my womb leaped for joy*: She is no longer carrying him; he is carrying her.

Beyond that, Elizabeth is given new gifts. Elizabeth was not a prophetess; yet once Our Lady enters her life, she is given the spirit of prophecy. She is the first to proclaim not only that the Messiah is present, but that he is the Son of God: *Who am I that the mother of my Lord should come to me?* Who told her that her young cousin was to be *mother of the Lord*, something of which even Joseph was ignorant? All of this happened through Mary's presence. So we are on scripturally sound terrain when we attest to the gifts of the Spirit that Our Lady poured into Mother Teresa, and when we declare these miracles of grace her reason for giving Our Lady "all her confidence."

Echoes of Our Lady in the Old Testament

Over the centuries Christian tradition has meditated on the many foreshadowings of the New Testament hidden in the Old, scattered across the pages of Scripture. Among these prophetic types, or symbols, we find the Jewish lamb of sacrifice, prefiguring Jesus as Lamb of God sacrificed on Calvary, and the manna in the desert, prefiguring the "true bread from heaven," the Eucharist. But especially in the Wisdom books of the Bible, there is also a foreshadowing of the person and the role of the Virgin Mary, prefigured in the Old Testament concept of *Wisdom,* presented as a person, and even as feminine, coming from God but distinct from him.[40]

Since there is a promised anointing on every Word of God — "My word . . . shall not return to me empty," as we read in Isaiah (55:11) — there is a special anointing of the spirit and grace given to these words of the Old Testament, which the Fathers of the Church saw as referring to Our Lady.

One way of entering into intimacy with her, of allowing her to play an active role in our lives, is to *listen* to her — to give her the chance to speak in our soul and to guide us, to become our "life coach" in the ways of the Lord, as she did for Juan Diego and for Mother Teresa.

These texts, sealed as they are with the Holy Sprit, are not offered for study, but for savoring. Take them a few lines at a time; turn them over in your soul — slowly. Invite her to take her place at your own Cana, at your own preparations for humanity's great wedding with the Lamb. Invite her to come, and she will come. Invite her to speak to your heart, through these words of Scripture, and she will speak — and your life will be changed, from this day forward. That this is true, Mother Teresa is the proof, the example, and the invitation.

From the Book of Proverbs

1:20-23

Wisdom cries aloud in the street;
    in the markets she raises her voice;
on the top of the walls she cries out;
    at the entrance of the city gates she speaks:
"How long, O simple ones, will you love being
    simple?
How long will scoffers delight in their scoffing
    and fools hate knowledge?
Give heed to my instruction;
behold, I will pour out my thoughts to you;
    I will make my words known to you."

2:1-5, 9-12

My son, if you receive my words
    and treasure up my instruction,
making your ear attentive to my wisdom
    and inclining your heart to understanding;
yes, if you long for insight

and raise your voice to ask for understanding,
if you seek it like silver
 and search for it as for hidden treasures;
then you will understand the fear of the LORD
 and come to the knowledge of God.
Then you will understand righteousness and justice
 and equity, and every good path;
for wisdom will enter your heart,
 and knowledge will gratify your soul;
discretion will watch over you;
 understanding will guard you;
delivering you from the way of evil,
 from men of perverted speech.

3:13-18

Happy is the one who finds wisdom,
 and the one who obtains understanding,
for its gain is better than silver
 and its profit better than gold.
She is more precious than jewels,
 and nothing you desire can compare with her.
Long life is in her right hand;
 in her left hand are riches and honor.
Her ways are pleasant,
 and all her paths are peace.
She is a tree of life to those who take hold of her;
 those who cling to her are blessed.

4:5-7, 8-13, 20-22

"Do not forget, and do not turn away from my words.

Find wisdom; seek insight.
Do not forsake her, and she will keep you;
    love her, and she will guard you.
The beginning of wisdom is this:
    Find wisdom.
Prize her highly, and she will exalt you;
    she will honor you if you embrace her.
She will place on your head a fair garland;
    she will bestow on you a beautiful crown."
Hear, my son, and accept my words,
    that the years of your life may be many.
I have taught you the way of wisdom;
    I have led you in the paths of uprightness.
When you walk, your step will not be hampered;
    and if you run, you will not stumble.
Keep hold of instruction, do not let go;
    guard her, for she is your life.
My son, be attentive to my words;
    incline your ear to my sayings.
Let them not escape from your sight;
    keep them within your heart.
For they are life to him who finds them,
    and healing to all his being.

7:1-4

My son, keep my words
    and treasure my commandments;
keep my commandments and live,
    keep my teachings as the apple of
        your eye;
bind them on your fingers,
    write them on the tablet of
        your heart.

Say to wisdom, "You are my sister,"
  and call insight your intimate friend.

8:1-6, 10-11, 14-21, 32-35

Does not wisdom call,
  does not understanding raise her voice?
On the heights beside the way,
  in the paths she takes her stand;
beside the gates in front of the town,
  at the entrance of the portals
    she cries aloud:
"To you I call,
  my cry is to the children of men.
O simple ones, learn prudence;
  O foolish men, pay heed.
Hear, for I will speak noble things,
  and from my lips will come what is right.
Value my instruction over silver,
  and knowledge over choice gold;
for wisdom is better than jewels,
  and all that you may desire cannot compare
    with her.
I give counsel and sound wisdom,
  insight, and strength.
By me kings reign,
  and rulers decree what is just;
by me princes rule,
  and nobles govern the earth.
I love those who love me,
  and those who seek me diligently find me.
Riches and honor are with me,
  enduring wealth and prosperity.
My fruit is better than gold, even fine gold,

and my yield than choice silver.
I walk in the way of righteousness,
    in the paths of justice,
endowing with wealth those who love me,
    and filling their treasuries.
And now, my children, listen to me:
    happy are those who keep my ways.
Hear instruction and be wise,
    and do not neglect it.
Happy is the one who listens to me,
    watching daily at my gates,
    waiting beside my doors.
For he who finds me finds life
    and obtains favor from the LORD."

9:1-5, 11

Wisdom has built her house,
    she has set up her seven pillars.
    She has set her table.
She has sent out her servants to call
    from the highest places in the town,
"Whoever is simple, let him turn in here!"
    To him who is without understanding
        she says,
"Come, eat of my bread
    and drink of the wine I have mixed."
For by me your days will be multiplied,
    and years will be added to your life.

From the Book of Wisdom

6:9, 11-20

To you then, O monarchs, my words
　　are directed,
that you may learn wisdom and not
　　transgress.
Therefore set your desire on my words;
long for them, and you will be instructed.
Wisdom is radiant and unfading,
　　and she is easily discerned by those who
　　　　love her,
and is found by those who seek her.
She hastens to make herself known to those
　　who desire her.
He who rises early to seek her will have
　　no difficulty,
for he will find her sitting at his gates.
To fix one's thought on her is perfect
　　understanding,
and he who is vigilant on her account will soon
　　be free from care,
because she goes about seeking those
　　worthy of her,
and she graciously appears to them in
　　their paths,
and meets them in every thought.
The beginning of wisdom is the most sincere
　　desire for instruction,
and concern for instruction is love of her,
and love of her is the keeping of her laws,
and giving heed to her laws is assurance of
　　immortality,
and immortality brings one near to God;

so the desire for wisdom leads
    to a kingdom.

7:7b-14, 22b-30

I called upon God, and the spirit of wisdom
    came to me.
I preferred her to scepters and thrones,
and I accounted wealth as nothing in
    comparison with her.
Neither did I liken to her any priceless gem,
because all gold is but a little sand in her sight,
and silver will be accounted as clay before her.
I loved her more than health and beauty,
and I chose to have her rather than light,
because her radiance never ceases.
All good things came to me along with her,
and in her hands uncounted wealth.
I rejoiced in them all, because wisdom
    leads them;
but I did not know that she was their mother.
I learned without guile and I impart
    without grudging;
I do not hide her wealth,
for it is an unfailing treasure for men;
those who find her obtain friendship
    with God.
For in her there is a spirit that is intelligent, holy,
unique, keen,
irresistible, beneficent,
steadfast, sure, free from anxiety,
all-powerful, overseeing all,
and penetrating through all spirits.
For wisdom is more mobile than any motion;

because of her pureness she pervades and
    penetrates all things.
For she is a breath of the power of God,
and a pure emanation of the glory of
    the Almighty;
therefore nothing defiled gains entrance
    into her.
For she is a reflection of eternal light,
a spotless mirror of the working of God,
and an image of his goodness.
Though she is but one, she can do all things,
and while remaining in herself, she renews
    all things;
in every generation she passes into holy souls
and makes them friends of God, and prophets;
for God loves nothing so much as the man who
    lives with wisdom.
For she is more beautiful than the sun,
and excels every constellation of the stars.
Compared with the light she is found to be
    superior,
for it is succeeded by the night,
but against wisdom evil does not prevail.

❦

8:1-2, 4-5, 7-10, 13, 16-18, 21

Wisdom reaches mightily from one end of the
    earth to the other,
and she orders all things well.
I loved her and sought her from my youth,
and I desired to take her for my bride,
and I became enamored of her beauty.
For she is an initiate in the knowledge of God,
and an associate in his works.

If riches are a desirable possession in life,
what is richer than wisdom who effects
    all things?
And if any one loves righteousness,
The fruit of her labor is virtue;
for she teaches self-control and prudence,
justice and courage;
nothing in life is more profitable for men
    than these.
And if any one longs for experience,
she knows the things of old, and infers the things
    to come;
she understands turns of speech and the solutions
    of riddles;
she has foreknowledge of signs and wonders
and of the outcome of seasons and times.
Therefore I determined to take her to live
    with me,
knowing that she would give me good counsel
and encouragement in cares and grief.
Because of her I shall have glory among
    the multitudes
and honor in the presence of the elders, though
    I am young.
Because of her I shall have immortality,
and leave an everlasting remembrance to those
    who come after me.
When I enter my house, I shall find rest
    with her,
for companionship with her has no bitterness,
and life with her has no pain, but gladness
    and joy.
When I considered these things inwardly,
and thought upon them in my mind,
that in kinship with wisdom there is immortality,

and in friendship with her, pure delight,
and in the labors of her hands, unfailing wealth,
and in the experience of her company,
    understanding,
and renown in sharing her words,
I went about seeking how to get her
    for myself.
But I perceived that I would not possess
    wisdom unless God gave her to me —
and it was a mark of insight to know whose
    gift she was —
so I appealed to the Lord and implored him.

9:10-11

Send her forth from the holy heavens,
and from the throne of thy glory send her,
that she may be with me in my toil,
and that I may learn what is pleasing to you.
For she knows and understands all things,
and she will guide me wisely in my actions
and guard me with her glory.

10:9-17

Wisdom rescued from troubles those who
    served her.
When a righteous man fled from his
    brother's wrath,
she guided him on straight paths;
she showed him the kingdom of God,
and gave him knowledge of angels;
she prospered him in his labors,

and increased the fruit of his toil.
When his oppressors were covetous,
she stood by him and made him rich.
She protected him from his enemies,
and kept him safe from those who lay
    in wait for him;
in his arduous contest she gave him the victory,
so that he might learn that godliness is more
    powerful than anything.
When a righteous man was sold, wisdom did
    not desert him,
but delivered him from sin.
She descended with him into the dungeon,
and when he was in prison she did not
    leave him,
until she brought him the scepter
    of a kingdom
and authority over his masters.
Those who accused him she showed
    to be false,
and she gave him everlasting honor.
A holy people and blameless race
wisdom delivered from a nation of oppressors.
She entered the soul of a servant of the Lord,
and withstood dread kings with wonders
    and signs.
She gave holy men the reward of their labors;
she guided them along a marvelous way,
and became a shelter to them by day,
and a starry flame through the night.

From the Book of Sirach

1:4, 5-7, 16-17

Wisdom was created before all things.
    And her ways are God's eternal commandments.
The root of wisdom — to whom has it been revealed?
    Her clever counsels — who knows them?
The knowledge of wisdom — to whom was it
        manifested?
    And her abundant experience — who has
        understood it?
    She satisfies men with her fruits;
she fills their whole house with desirable goods,
    and their storehouses with her produce.

4:11-17, 18

Wisdom breathes life into her children
    and gives help to those who seek her.
Whoever loves her loves life,
    and those who seek her early
    will win the Lord's good favor.
Whoever holds her fast will obtain glory,
    and the Lord will bless the place she enters.
Those who serve her minister to the Holy One;
the Lord loves those who love her.
He who obeys her will judge the nations,
    and whoever gives heed to her will dwell secure.
If he has faith in her he will obtain her;
    and his descendants will remain in possession
        of her.
For she will walk with him hiddenly,
    And at first she will put him to the test,
    until he holds her in his thoughts.

Then she will come to him and strengthen him,
    she will gladden him and will reveal her
        secrets to him,
    and store up for him knowledge
    and the discernment of what is right.

6:18-19, 23-31

My child, from your youth choose instruction,
    and until you are old you will keep finding
        wisdom.
Come to her like one who plows and sows,
    and wait for her good harvest.
For in her service you will toil a little while,
    and soon you will eat of her produce.
Listen, my son, and accept my judgment;
    do not reject my counsel.
Put your feet into her chains,
    and your neck into her collar.
Put your shoulder under her and carry her,
    and do not fret under her bonds.
Come to her with all your soul,
    and keep her ways with all your might.
Search out and seek, and she will become known
    to you;
    and when you get hold of her, do not let
        her go.
For at last you will find the rest she gives,
    and she will be changed into joy for you.
Then her fetters will become for you
    a strong protection,
and her collar a glorious robe.
Her yoke is a golden ornament,
    and her bonds are a cord of royal blue.

You will wear her like a glorious robe,
    and put her on like a crown of gladness.

24:1-3, 4, 7-21, 27-31

Wisdom will glory in the midst of her people.
In the assembly of the Most High she will open
        her mouth,
    and in the presence of his host she will glory:
In the midst of her people she is exalted;
    in the holy fullness she is admired.
In the multitude of the chosen she finds praise,
    and among the blessed she is blessed, saying:
"I came forth from the mouth of the Most High,
    The first-born before all creatures.
I dwelt in high places,
    and my throne was in a pillar of cloud.
Among all these I sought a resting place;
    I sought in whose territory I might lodge.
"Then the Creator of all things gave me a
        commandment,
    and the one who created me assigned a
        place for my tent.
And he said, 'Make your dwelling in Jacob,
    and in Israel receive your inheritance,
    and among my chosen put down your roots.'
From eternity, in the beginning, he created me,
    and for eternity I shall not cease to exist.
In the holy tabernacle I ministered before him,
    and so I was established in Zion.
In the beloved city likewise he gave me a resting place,
    and in Jerusalem was my dominion.
So I took root in an honored people,

in the portion of the Lord, who is their
   inheritance,
   and my abode was in the full assembly
      of the saints.
"I grew tall like a cedar in Lebanon,
   and like a cypress on the heights of
      Hermon.
I grew tall like a palm tree in En-gedi,
   and like rose plants in Jericho;
like a beautiful olive tree in the field,
   and like a plane tree I grew tall.
Like cassia and camel's thorn I gave forth the
      aroma of spices,
   and like choice myrrh I spread a pleasant odor,
      like the fragrance of frankincense in the
         tabernacle.
Like a terebinth I spread out my branches,
   and my branches are glorious and graceful.
Like a vine I caused loveliness to bud,
   and my blossoms became glorious and
      abundant fruit.
"Come to me, you who desire me,
   and eat your fill of my produce.
For my teaching is sweeter than honey,
   and my inheritance sweeter than the
      honeycomb,
   and my remembrance lasts throughout all
      generations.
Those who eat me will hunger for more,
   and those who drink me will thirst for more."
She makes instruction shine forth like light,
   like the Gihon at the time of vintage.
Just as the first man did not know her perfectly,
   the last one has not fathomed her;
for her thought is more abundant than the sea,

and her counsel deeper than the great abyss.
I went forth like a canal from a river
    and like a water channel into a garden.
I said, "I will water my orchard
    and drench my garden plot";
    and behold, my canal became a river,
    and my river became a sea.

51:13-16, 18-21, 25b-27

While I was still young, before I went on my
        travels,
    I sought wisdom openly in my prayer.
Before the temple I asked for her,
    and I will search for her to the last.
From blossom to ripening grape
    my heart delighted in her;
my foot entered upon the straight path;
    from my youth I followed her steps.
I inclined my ear a little and received her,
    and I found for myself much instruction.
For I resolved to live according to wisdom,
    and I was zealous for the good;
    and I shall never be put to shame.
My soul clung to wisdom;
I spread out my hands to the heavens,
    and lamented my ignorance of her.
I directed my soul to her,
    and through purification I found her.
I gained understanding with her from the first,
    therefore I will not be forsaken.
My heart was stirred to seek her,
    therefore I have gained a good possession.
    Get these things for yourselves without money.

Put your neck under the yoke,
    and let your souls receive instruction;
    she is to be found close by.
See with your eyes that I have labored little
    and found myself much rest.

Appendix Three

Nican Mopohua:
The Story of Juan Diego

All written narrations about the apparitions of the Lady of Guadalupe are inspired by the Nican Mopohua, *written in Nahuatl, the Aztec language, by the Indian scholar Antonio Valeriano around the middle of the sixteenth century. A copy was first published by Luis Lasso de la Vega in 1649.*

COVER OF THE LASSO DE LA VEGA BOOK, 1649

Here follows a paraphrase of Valeriano's work.

Ten years after the seizure of the city of Mexico, war came to an end and there was peace among the people. Faith, the understanding of the true God, started to blossom. It was in December of the year 1531 that a poor Indian named Juan Diego had a remarkable encounter.

The First Apparition

On a Saturday just before dawn, Juan Diego was on his way to Divine Worship. When he reached the base of the hill called Tepeyac, he heard singing coming from the hill, like the singing of beautiful birds only even more beautiful. Juan Diego stopped and said to himself: "Am I worthy of what I hear? Am I dreaming, or am I waking up? Where am I? Could it be that I have reached the terrestrial paradise which our elders told us about? Am I in heaven?" As he was looking toward the east, toward the top of the hill, the singing suddenly ceased and all became silent. He then heard a voice calling to him: "My little Juan, my little Juan Diego." He went toward the voice, not in fear but in great joy.

When he reached the top, he saw a Lady, who told him to approach. As he drew near, he was amazed at her heavenly beauty. Her clothing shone like the sun, and the place where she stood sparkled like a rainbow. The plants around her seemed to glisten like precious gems. Juan Diego bowed before her, and she spoke gently and courteously to him.

"Juanito, littlest of my sons, where are you going?"

He answered, "My Lady, I am going to your church to pursue the things of God."

She said to him:

"Know, littlest of my sons, that I am the ever-virgin Holy Mary, Mother of the True God by whom we live, of the Creator of all things, Lord of heaven and earth. I desire that a temple be built here soon so that I may show all my love, my compassion, my help, and my protection, because I am your merciful mother; yours, and of all the inhabitants in this land, of all who love me. There I will hear their sorrows and remedy all their afflictions. Go then to the bishop of Mexico, and tell him all you have seen and heard. I will be grateful and will reward you with happiness. See, you have heard my command, my littlest son; go and put forth all your effort."

Juan Diego bowed before her and said: "My Lady, I will obey your command. I must go now, your humble servant." He went back down the hill and took the road to Mexico City.

The Second Apparition

Juan Diego entered the city and went straight to the bishop's palace. He pleaded with the servants to announce him, and after a long wait, he was called in to see the bishop, a Franciscan named Juan de Zumarraga, who had recently arrived in Mexico City. He entered and bowed, and then delivered the message from the heavenly Lady, along with everything he had seen and heard. The bishop was polite to him and told him that he would hear him again another time. But Juan Diego was sad, since it appeared that the bishop did not plan to act on the message.

Juan Diego returned to the hill of Tepeyac on the same day. He went to the top of the hill and found the heavenly Lady waiting for him at the same spot where he had first seen her. He bowed before her and said:

"Lady, I did what you commanded. With difficulty I entered the bishop's study. I gave him your message, just as you instructed me. He received me kindly and listened attentively, but it seemed as though he did not believe me. I understood by the manner of his answer that he thinks that this matter of a temple to be built in your honor is an invention of mine. I beg you, Lady, to entrust your message to someone important and well known, someone they might believe. I am no one, nothing, and I know nothing of the bishop's palace. Please do not be angry with me, my Lady."

The Blessed Virgin answered:

"Least of my sons, you must understand that I have many servants and messengers; but it is of great importance that you be the one to take this message. Go back again tomorrow and see the bishop. You go in my name; tell him that the ever-virgin Mary, Mother of God, has sent you."

Juan Diego replied:

"Lady, I will gladly obey, and will not fail, though I may not be believed. I will come back tomorrow afternoon at sunset, and bring you the bishop's answer."

With that he departed for home.

The Third Apparition

The next day, Sunday, Juan Diego left his home before dawn to go to Divine Worship, following which he was to see the bishop. After hearing Mass, he arrived at the bishop's palace, and once again, with much difficulty, he was admitted. He knelt before the bishop and told him again of the command of the heavenly Lady, that a temple be built on the hill to her honor. The bishop asked about the Lady, where he had seen her, and how she looked. Nonetheless, he did not comply with the command. He said he needed a sign to be sure that this was truly the Blessed Virgin.

Juan Diego answered, "What sign do you seek? I will go to the heavenly Lady and ask it from her." The bishop then dismissed him, and he sent some trusted members of his household to follow Juan Diego and see what he would do and to whom he would speak. But they lost sight of him, and they returned greatly annoyed at not having been able to follow him. They told the bishop that Juan Diego was either lying or dreaming. They further planned to take him and punish him if he were ever to return, in order to cure him of his lying.

Meanwhile Juan Diego returned to the Blessed Virgin, and told her the answer the bishop gave him. The heavenly Lady responded:

> "Very well, my dear little one, return here tomorrow, so that you may take to the bishop the sign he has asked for. Then he will believe you and will no longer be suspicious of you. And I will reward you for your efforts in my behalf. Go! I will be waiting for you here tomorrow."

The Fourth Apparition

On the following day, Monday, Juan Diego did not return to the hill, because his uncle, Juan Bernardino, had become gravely ill. Juan Diego sent for the doctor, but it seemed to be too late. That night his uncle requested of him that he go the next morning to summon a priest, to prepare him for death and hear his confession, because he was certain that his time had come.

On Tuesday before dawn, Juan Diego left his home on this errand. When he came to the road that went toward the hill of Tepeyac, he said to himself: "If I go this way, the Lady is bound to see me and detain me for the sign I must take to the bishop." So he went the other way around the hill. Nonetheless, the heavenly Lady came to him as he skirted the hill and said to him: "Where are you going, my littlest son?" He bowed before her, not knowing if he was more grieved or frightened. He said to her:

"My Lady, God grant that you are happy. How are you this morning? Is your health good, Lady? A servant of yours, my uncle, has contracted the plague and is near death. I am hurrying to your house in Mexico to call one of your beloved priests to hear his confession and absolve him. But I will return here soon, so that I may deliver your message. My Lady, forgive me, be patient with me. Tomorrow I will come quickly."

The Most Holy Virgin answered:

"My littlest son, let nothing frighten or grieve you. Let not your heart be disturbed. Do not fear this sickness, nor any sickness or suffering. Am I not here, I who am your Mother? Are you not in my shadow, under my protection? Am I not your health? Are you not happily within my fold? What else do you wish? Do not grieve or be disturbed by anything. Do not be afflicted by the illness of your uncle, who will not die of it. Be assured that he is now cured."

And so it was that at that moment his uncle was cured, as was later discovered.

When Juan Diego heard these words, he was greatly comforted. In his happiness he begged to be allowed to go see the bishop with the sign that would allow his words to be believed. The heavenly Lady said to him: "Climb, my least son, to the top of the hill where you first saw me. There you will find flowers. Cut them and gather them together and bring them to me."

Juan Diego climbed the hill, and was amazed to find there many varieties of exquisite Castilian roses, fragrant and in full bloom, though it was winter. At once he began cutting them, and he gathered them and placed them in his *tilma*. The hilltop was no place for flowers; it had many thistles, thorns, and cactus plants. Not even weeds would grow there in the cold month of December. Juan Diego went back down the hill with the roses he had cut and brought them to the heavenly Lady. She took them and placed them back in the *tilma*, and said:

"My littlest son, these roses are the sign you are to take to the bishop. Tell him in my name to comply with my wishes. But only in the presence of the bishop shall you unfold your mantle and show what it is you are carrying. Tell him all that you have seen and done on my orders, and tell him once again to erect a temple as I have asked."

Juan Diego, happy and confident, went his way directly to Mexico City, taking great care that nothing would slip from his *tilma*, and enjoying the fragrance of the beautiful roses.

The Miracle of the Image

When Juan Diego reached the bishop's palace, he begged to be taken to the bishop. But the servants pretended not to hear him, thinking him to be a bother, and influenced by what they had been told by those who had followed him earlier. When they saw that he was standing a long time, crestfallen, doing nothing, waiting to be called, and that he seemed to be carrying something in his *tilma*, they approached him to see what it was. Juan Diego saw that he could not hide what he was carrying, and so to avoid violence against him, he uncovered the edge of his *tilma*. There were the fresh Castilian roses, fragrant, beautiful, in full bloom. The men were amazed, and tried to seize the flowers and pull them out of the *tilma*. Three times they tried, but they were not successful, and the flowers seemed to become nothing more than a painted image. Then they went to tell the bishop that the Indian who had come so many times before wished to see him again, and that he had something to show him.

When the bishop heard this, he realized that Juan Diego was bringing the sign he had requested. He immediately ordered his admission. Juan Diego knelt before him as he was accustomed to do, and again told him all that he had seen:

> "Sir, I did what you ordered. I went to the heavenly Lady, Holy Mary, the precious Mother of God, and told her that you asked for a sign, that you might believe her wish. She has graciously

granted your request. Early today she sent me to the top of the hill where I was accustomed to see her, and told me to cut the Castilian roses I found there. After I had cut them, I brought them to her, and she took them with her hand and placed them in my cloth, that I might deliver them to you in person. I knew that the hilltop was no place for flowers. But as I approached the top of the hill, I saw that I was in Paradise, surrounded by exquisite flowers. I was told to bring them to you so that you may see in them the sign you requested and believe my message. Behold. Receive them."

Juan Diego unfolded the cloth that was holding the flowers, and as all the different varieties of Castilian roses scattered on the floor, there suddenly appeared the precious Image of the ever-virgin Holy Mary, Mother of God, just as she is today kept in the temple at Tepeyac, which is named Guadalupe. When the bishop saw the image, he and all who were present fell to their knees. The bishop, with sorrowful tears, prayed and begged forgiveness for not having attended to her wish and request. When he rose to his feet, he untied the cloth with the Image of the Lady from heaven from Juan Diego's neck. Then he took it to be placed in his chapel. Juan Diego remained one more day in the bishop's house, at his request.

The following day the bishop said to him, "Come! Show us where the Lady from heaven wished her temple to be erected." And he invited all those present to go along.

The Apparition to Juan Bernardino

Juan Diego brought the bishop to the spot where the heavenly Lady wanted her temple built, but he then begged to be excused. He wanted to see his uncle Juan

Bernardino, who had still been gravely ill when he had left him that morning. But they did not let him go alone; they all accompanied him to his home.

Upon their arrival, they found Juan Bernardino happy and healthy. He was amazed to see his nephew so accompanied and honored, and he asked the reason. His nephew then told him of the vision at Tepeyac, that the heavenly Lady had told him that his uncle would be healed, and that he should go to the bishop with the message that he was to build a house for her. Then Juan Diego's uncle revealed that he also had seen the heavenly Lady just as she had appeared to his nephew, and that she had cured him. The Lady told him to relate to the bishop his miraculous cure, and to say that she was to be named the Virgin Mary of Guadalupe.

Juan Diego and his uncle Juan Bernardino were guests of the bishop for many days, until the temple dedicated to the Queen of Tepeyac was erected upon the spot where Juan Diego had seen her. The bishop transferred the sacred Image of the heavenly Lady to the main church, so that all the people could see and venerate her blessed Image. The entire city was very moved; they came to see and to venerate the Image, and to pray. They marveled at this divine miracle, because no person of this world had painted her precious Image.

Notes

[1] Mother Teresa's Instructions to the M.C. Sisters, Tijuana, January 1992.

[2] Brian Kolodiejchuk, M.C., *Mother Teresa: Come Be My Light* (New York: Doubleday, 2007), p. 1.

[3] See *La Noche Oscura* in *Complete Works of John of the Cross*.

[4] Mother's Letters (hereafter ML): 6.3.62.

[5] Brian Kolodiejchuk, M.C., *Mother Teresa: Come Be My Light* (New York: Doubleday, 2007), p. 99.

[6] Brian Kolodiejchuk, M.C., *Mother Teresa: Come Be My Light* (New York: Doubleday, 2007), p. 99.

[7] Mother's Instructions (hereafter MI): March 7,1979.

[8] MI: September 29, 1977.

[9] Brian Kolodiejchuk, M.C., *Mother Teresa: Come Be My Light* (New York: Doubleday, 2007), p. 98.

[10] Mother Teresa to the M.C. Sisters, April 2, 1987.

[11] ML: July 31, 1996.

[12] Mother Teresa's Instructions to the Novice Mistresses, Casilina/Rome, June 30, 1997.

[13] Mother Teresa to the M.C. Sisters, April 24, 1996.

[14] Original Rule Explanation, #4.

[15] Mother Teresa to the M.C. Sisters, July 31, 1996.

[16] Original Rule Explanation, #4.

[17] Mother Teresa's Instructions to the M.C. Sisters, February 15, 1997.

[18] Mother Teresa's Speech to Youth, Naples, May 11, 1996.

[19] Another term for "Congregation."

[20] Mother Teresa to the M.C. Sisters, July 31, 1996.

[21] Mother Teresa to the M.C. Sisters, March 6, 1992.

[22] Mother Teresa to the M.C. Sisters, September 5, 1997.

[23] Testimony of an M.C. Sister.

[24] Mother Teresa to the M.C. Sisters, March 14, 1997.

[25] Brian Kolodiejchuk, M.C., *Mother Teresa: Come Be My Light* (New York: Doubleday, 2007), p. 99.

[26] *Rosarium Virginis Mariae* (October 16, 2002), no. 12. Emphasis in original.

[27] Original Rule Explanation, #4.

[28] Mother Teresa to the M.C. Sisters, June 18, 1972.

[29] Angelus meditation (July 24, 1988).

[30] Mother Teresa to the M.C. Sisters, August 1992.

[31] Missionaries of Charity, *Prayerbook*.

[32] Mother Teresa's Instructions to the M.C. Sisters.

[33] Testimony of an M.C. Sister.

[34] Testimony of an M.C. Sister.

[35] Mother Teresa to the M.C. Sisters, November 15, 1996.

[36] Original Rule Explanation, #4.

[37] Original Rule Explanation, #4.

[38] Andrew of Crete, *Sermon I on the Birth of Mary*, as quoted in Pope John Paul II, "Mary Was Conceived Without Original Sin," *L'Osservatore Romano* (May 22, 1996), p. 11.

[39] *Rosarium Virginis Mariae* (October 16, 2002), no. 16.

[40] Including the books of Job, Proverbs, Ecclesiastes, and Song of Songs, as well as the Deuterocanonical books of Sirach and Wisdom. The Scripture verses in this appendix are adapted from the *Second Catholic Edition of the Revised Standard Version of the Bible* (RSV).

Acknowledgments

Scripture excerpts are taken from the following translations:

- The *Second Catholic Edition of the Revised Standard Version of the Bible* (RSV), copyright © 1965, 1966, and 2006 by the Division of Christian Education of the National Council of the Churches of Christ in the United States of America. Used by permission. All rights reserved.
- The *New American Bible with Revised New Testament and Psalms* (NAB) copyright © 1991, 1986, 1970, Confraternity of Christian Doctrine, Inc., Washington, D.C. Used with permission. All rights reserved.
- The *Holy Bible, New International Version*® (NIV). Copyright © 1973, 1978, 1984 by International Bible Society. Used by permission of Zondervan Publishing House. All rights reserved.

Unless otherwise noted, English translations of papal and other Vatican documents are from the Vatican website, www.vatican.va.

Mother Teresa's words © 2007 Missionaries of Charity Sisters, c/o Mother Teresa Center. Used with permission.

About the Author

Joseph Langford, MC, began his long association with Mother Teresa while studying theology in Rome. In 1983, she invited him to be the co-founder of her priests' community, the Missionaries of Charity Fathers. He resides at the community's motherhouse in Tijuana, Mexico, where he can be contacted at frjosephmc.book@yahoo.com.

Our Lady of Guadalupe